CW00493910

The Religion of Art

For thirty years, Sangharakshita has been playing an important part in the spread of Buddhism throughout the modern world. He is head of the Western Buddhist Order (Trailokya Bauddha Mahasangha), and is actively engaged in the development of what is now an international Buddhist movement with centres in thirteen countries worldwide. When not visiting centres he is based at a community in Norfolk. His writings are available in eleven languages.

Also by Sangharakshita:

Messengers from Tibet and Other Poems
A Survey of Buddhism
Flame in Darkness
The Enchanted Heart
The Three Jewels
The Essence of Zen
The Path of the Inner Life
The Thousand-Petalled Lotus
Human Enlightenment
The Ten Pillars of Buddhism
The Eternal Legacy
Travel Letters
Alternative Traditions
Conquering New Worlds
Ambedkar and Buddhism
Crossing the Stream

The Meaning of Orthodoxy in Buddhism
Mind—Reactive and Creative
Aspects of Buddhist Morality
Buddhism and Blasphemy
Buddhism, World Peace, and Nuclear War
The Bodhisattva: Evolution and Self-Transcendence
The Glory of the Literary World
Going For Refuge
The Caves of Bhaja

The Religion of Art

Sangharakshita

Windhorse Publications

Windhorse Publications
136 Renfield Street
Glasgow G2 3AU

© Windhorse Publications 1988

ISBN 0 904766 31 4

The Meaning of Buddhism and the Value of Art was first published in 1956 by the Maha Bodhi Society under the title *Buddhism and Art. The Religion of Art* was first published in 1973 by The Arya Maitreya Mandala in a book celebrating the 75th birthday of Lama Anagarika Govinda. *Paradox and Poetry in 'The Voice of the Silence'* was first published in 1958 by the Indian Institute of World Culture. *Advice to a Young Poet* was first published in *The Aryan Path (1953, two issues).*

Cover design by Dharmachari Dhammarati. The vase painting shows 'Orpheus among the Thracians', and is reproduced with the kind permission of the British Museum.

The poem, 'After Rilke' appears in *Conquering New Worlds*, also published by Windhorse.

Printed by F. Crowe & Sons Ltd, 11 Concorde Road, Norwich, Norfolk, NR6 6BJ

Contents

Introduction

We know from reading Sangharakshita's volume of memoirs, *The Thousand-Petalled Lotus*, that at the age of twenty-one, having been drafted out to India during the war, and the war having ended, he left the army, and donned the bright ochre garb of an ascetic. He wandered, together with a friend, the highways and byways of South India in search of the truth for two and a half years, meeting many eminent Hindu swamis, such as the famous Ramana Maharshi and Ramdas. After this period of wandering Sangharakshita spent seven months at Benares University studying Pali, Abidharma, and Logic under Bhikkhu Kashyap, or Kashyapji, as he was generally known.

It was during these years that he became conscious of a conflict between contradictory parts of himself, which in *The Thousand-Petalled Lotus* he calls Sangharakshita I and Sangharakshita II. 'Sangharakshita I wanted to enjoy the beauty of nature, to read and write poetry, to listen to music, to look at paintings and sculpture, to experience emotion, to lie in bed and dream, to see places, to meet people. Sangharakshita II wanted to realize the truth, to read and write philosophy, to observe the precepts, to get up early and meditate, to mortify the flesh, to fast and pray'.

During this period of wandering, Sangharakshita II had 'ruled practically unchallenged', and Sangharakshita I been almost completely denied. Indeed the latter could have died altogether were it not for the timely intervention of Swami Ramdas, who firmly declared that writing poetry was *not* incompatible with the spiritual life.

It was perhaps the eventual resolution of this conflict which was to give birth to the four essays republished here, all of which date back to a particular period between 1953 and 1954, when Sangharakshita was staying in Kalimpong.

Kalimpong is a small town in the foothills of the eastern Himalayas, and at that time, before the Chinese invasion of Tibet, was a very busy and prosperous place, conveniently situated on the Indo-Tibetan border, and on the Tibetan trade route. Sangharakshita had been left there, one brilliantly sunny March day in 1950, by Kashyapji, who told him to stay and 'work for the good of Buddhism'. The scenery and atmosphere of Kalimpong had made a deep impression on the young English novice Buddhist monk, and he was happy to stay on in such an inspiring and magical place. At the age of twenty-four, he found himself alone for the first time in his life.

After living for short periods elsewhere in Kalimpong, Sangharakshita moved to a five-roomed bungalow which became known as 'The Hermitage'. When he first took up residence, it was in a semi-derelict condition, not having been lived in for many years. Light shone in through chinks in the walls, and the earth could be seen through the gaps between the floorboards. It was a simple wood-frame structure with a corrugated iron roof that let the rain in in places. There was not much furniture—just a rickety old table and chair and a broken book-case. It was here that Sangharakshita wrote the four essays in this book.

The Hermitage had a beautiful, though sadly neglected, garden. In it there was an octagonal-shaped summer-house, which Sangharakshita used as a meditation-room. In front of the summer-house there was a circular pond, and leading up to the pond a gravel path. He used to spend hours just walking up and down the path, thinking, reflecting, meditating—he composed many poems in this way. The garden itself contained many beautiful ornamental trees—magnolias, chocolate palms, tulip trees, camellias, and an abundance of bamboo orchids. Sangharakshita was enchanted by the place.

From his poems of that period (in Sangharakshita's own words his poems constitute a sort of spiritual autobiography), and from his memoirs of the same period, it seems that 'The Religion of Art' was written at a time of intense spiritual activity: both internally, in terms of his own meditations—as can be seen in his poem 'Up and Down the Gravel Path'—and externally in his work for Buddhism. He founded, edited, and published *Stepping Stones,* 'a monthly magazine of Himalayan religion, culture and education', which though short-lived was to have a wide influence on the Buddhist world, and would inspire contributions from an ever-growing circle of friends, such as Lama Govinda, Dr Herbert Guenther, Prince Peter of Greece, George Roerich, and Marco Pallis. He also set up at The Hermitage the Kalimpong Young Men's Buddhist Association, where, in addition to giving lectures and educational film-shows, he provided extra tuition to help the local boys with their school work.

The beauty of the Himalayan scenery had a profound impact on him. It reawakened his interest in literature and poetry, and it gave him great inspiration in his own writing. He rediscovered the work of D. H. Lawrence, whose novel *The Rainbow* had made such a deep impression on him in his youth. Other formative influences on him at this time were Herbert Read's *The Meaning of Art* and the poetry of Baudelaire, Yeats, and Tagore, whose *Stray Birds,* discovered in a bookshop in Darjeeling, was to influence the poetic form of Sangharakshita's own poem *The Veil of Stars*.

'The Religion of Art' in fact seems to have been written just after *The Veil of Stars*. Perhaps 'The Religion of Art' can be seen as a sort of commentary to that poem—it is certainly useful to read the two works in conjunction with one another. Although that wasn't necessarily the author's intention, the two works do seem to have grown out of the same underlying spiritual experience: an awakening of the heart, touched off by a deep response to beauty. And they both undeniably reflect the philosophy of emotion, intellectual and spiritual vigour, and surety in spiritual values, that enabled him to bring that awakening about. At the time of writing 'The Religion of Art', Sangharakshita felt inspired to write about things that interested him, not things that other people wanted him to write: it is probably the most spontaneous prose piece he has ever written. The essay remained unpublished for over twenty years.

'The Religion of Art' is a manifesto. It advocates a religion of beauty. It argues that true art is a means to the communication of spiritual values, and that in this it performs the same function as religion. When confronted with the work of art, if we are open to it, we are compelled to change our lives in accordance with it—to assimilate an experience which is at once powerful and refined, intensely real, and wholly unfamiliar to us. It is precisely this province with which religion, too, is concerned: the expansion of consciousness, the heightening of awareness, the experiencing of what Wordsworth called 'unknown modes of being'. Religion and art can be seen as complementary aspects—reason and emotion—of the same process of higher human development. It is this insight, perhaps more than any other, which informs the pages of these four essays.

It was in fact while giving tuition to his students at The Hermitage on a poem by Shelley that Sangharakshita had this insight—that Buddhism and true art are essentially one and the same thing. Perhaps one could say that it was in this moment that Sangharakshitas I and II, after many years of uneasy coexistence, finally married and gave birth to

Sangharakshita III, who 'united beauty and truth, poetry and philosophy, spontaneity and discipline'. And the essays in this volume perhaps represent the outward expression of this marriage, the working out of this insight.

With Buddhism now growing rapidly in the West, it is of particular interest that Sangharakshita illustrates his thesis with examples from Western art, referring for instance to Shelley, Rilke, and D. H. Lawrence. Indeed, these essays not only show the connection between religion and art, but in effect also reveal a bridge between Buddhism and Western culture. In these early essays we see Sangharakshita perhaps for the first time trying to teach Buddhism—to communicate the spirit of the Dharma—in terms of Western rather than Eastern culture. We see ideas and insights that were later to find concrete expression in his setting up of the Friends of the Western Buddhist Order in London in the late sixties. The FWBO seeks not merely to import Buddhism's Eastern cultural forms, but to go back two and a half thousand years to the original teaching of the Buddha—to discern, at the heart of all the various traditions of oriental Buddhism, the essential principles of the Dharma; and then to translate them faithfully, to re-express them in terms relevant to Western thought and culture. Sangharakshita has seen that if Buddhism is genuinely to take root in the West, this process of interpretation is vital. Like the figure of St Jerome in his essay *St Jerome Revisited*, Sangharakshita is a 'translator': indeed he can possibly be seen as one of the greatest modern-day translators of Buddhism. Perhaps, then, it is time to refer to him no longer as Sangharakshita III, but to use a name given to him by Khechu Rimpoche, one of his Tibetan teachers, and call him Urgyen Sangharakshita, Urgyen being one of the names of another great interpreter of the Dharma, Padmasambhava, the eighth century Indian guru who took Buddhism from India to Tibet.

In the winter of 1987, while I was on a visit to Sangharakshita at 'Padmaloka', where he lives, in Norfolk, he allowed me to read the typescript of his latest volume of memoirs, which when complete will deal with the period 1950—57, the first seven years of his fourteen-year sojourn in Kalimpong. While reading the typescript in the library, I was at one point overcome with a deep tiredness. Upon closing my eyes, quite unpremeditated, I saw before my mind's eye, emerging out of the darkness, a vision of the two bright red volumes of *The Life and Liberation of Padmasambhava*. It was only later that I realized that, reading the memoirs, in a sense I was reading *The Life and Liberation*—that is, that I had contacted something of that same spiritual current, that same magic, that colours the biography of that great teacher, with whom, I know, Sangharakshita feels such a deep affinity.

I spent several days immersed in the memoirs. The world of Kalimpong, Darjeeling, Nepal, and Sikkim in the early 1950s—the backdrop against which Sangharakshita wrote the four essays republished here—is so vividly conjured up in the memoirs that I felt that I too was living in that world.

At the end of my visit I travelled back to London in the train. As I gazed out of the window at the fields and trees, all glittering in hoar-frost, flashing past, I was still very much absorbed in the world of Sangharakshita's Himalayan journal. A phrase came into my mind, which I noted down: 'leaving Padmaloka this time felt like coming down from a magic mountain' . . . although somehow I had a sense of retaining something of that world of The Hermitage, the gravel path and the bamboo orchids—something very precious—and bringing it back to this world. It is my deep-felt desire that I should always stay in contact with that precious thing; and that this edition of the essays will enable many more people to gain access to it.

Padmaraja

'Rivendell'
Winter 1987—88.

After Rilke

The poet is the world's interpreter,
At least to his own self. He recreates
In his own heart the things he contemplates,
And brings them forth transformed from what they were
Into a beauty-truth that cannot err,
That cannot fade or die. Though dull ingrates
May mock, no vile disparagement abates
The benefits the poet's words confer.

A tree is not a tree, unless within
The poet's all-transmuting mind it grows
Refined, reborn,—by his own power redeemed
Into a truer life. The poet's kin
Are Memnon, Orpheus, Merlin. History shows
The best but live what once the poet dreamed.

The Meaning of Buddhism and the Value of Art

The Meaning of Buddhism and the Value of Art

It was about a century ago that Schopenhauer, who, more deeply than any other Western thinker, was influenced by, and imbued with, the spirit of ancient Indian philosophy, ventured to predict that the renaissance that would be brought about by the discovery, in the nineteenth century, of the treasures of oriental literature, would be incomparably more glorious than that which had been ushered in during the fifteenth and sixteenth centuries by the rediscovery of the classics of Greece and Rome. This bold prediction of the nineteenth century is being fulfilled, or at least beginning to be fulfilled, in the twentieth. What was merely political and commercial contact between the nations of the East and the West has begun to deepen into cultural exchanges and interreligious fellowship. Throughout every Western land, men and women are now to be found—few in number, indeed, but increasingly influential— who are convinced that now as ever light comes from the East: *Ex Oriente lux*.

Of the rays into which that light, shooting through the spectrum of human understanding, is broken up, none confronts occidental eyes with a steadier radiance, or shines forth with a more blindingly brilliant effulgence, than the hitherto unknown splendour to which the West, startled into awareness of a whole new world of values, has given the name 'Buddhism'. Yet often is that splendour dimmed by the opacity of the medium through which it is transmitted. Even today, when the Pali Text Society of London and other bodies, as well as distinguished scholars working independently in the field of Buddhist studies, have between them published a small library of Pali, Sanskrit, Chinese, and Tibetan Buddhist texts and their translations, the writers of articles and compilers of popular handbooks on Buddhism, ignoring this mass of authentic material, are frequently found repeating the same old misunderstandings about Nirvana and other points of Buddhist doctrine.

Such misunderstandings, when they are not due to ineradicable religious prejudice, such as still animates many Christian writers on non-Christian religions, may be traced to a misconception of the very nature of Buddhism. This misconception has its roots deep down in the history of Western thought. Briefly stated, it consists in regarding Buddhism as a system of philosophy in the modern academic sense.

To the ancient Greeks and Romans, philosophy was not merely an opinion, but a passion; it meant not only loftier thinking, but nobler living. A philosopher was expected to leave his hair and beard untrimmed, to wear but one long simple garment, to sleep on the bare ground, and to eat sparingly. With the irruption of Christianity into the Graeco-Roman world, the old classic ideals of moderation, balance, and harmony were destroyed. Wisdom was replaced by faith, while for the harmless and helpful philosophic life was substituted one of aggressive good works (which included the conversion of the heathen, by force, if necessary, and the burning of heretics). Between faith and works some kind of harmony was indeed sought to be maintained, but, covering as these did only a small part of the scale of human potentialities, this harmony was not rich or full enough to be long sustained, and, before many centuries had passed, the shrill note of faith first dominated and then drowned all others.

The modern scientific attitude of mind developed in part as a protest against the unverifiable dogmas of medieval Christianity, and every advance in scientific knowledge was made in the teeth of determined ecclesiastical opposition; for the schoolman, no less than the scientist, was aware that the victory of science spelled the defeat of faith. With the abandonment of Christian doctrine came the tacit repudiation of the Christian way of life, and though individual thinkers continued to conform to Christian ethical standards and even, in some cases, professed to accept the Christian revelation, Western thought came more and more under the influence of science and developed with increasing freedom from religious preconceptions. The introduction of psychological and epistemological interests strengthened still further the theoretical and speculative tendencies in modern thought, and, by the time Schopenhauer arose to challenge the academic and professorial conception of philosophy, despite artificial attempts at reconciliation the divorce between religion and philosophy had been made absolute.

A division between concrete living and abstract thinking continues to characterize modern Western culture. Philosophy is taught at universities as a purely theoretical subject; it does not demand from its votaries the adoption of a distinctive mode of life, neither does it have as a whole any bearing upon practical affairs. For the philosophic life, as it was understood by the Greeks and Romans in even their most degenerate days—the passionate pursuit of beauty, truth, and goodness, and the endeavour to reflect them in one's own life—has been substituted the detached and barren study of the history of philosophical opinions.

When the star of Buddhism first rose above these icy academic horizons, its dependence on reason rather than faith, its freedom from credulity and superstition, not unnaturally caused it to be regarded as an ethicophilosophical system rather than as a religion in the Christian sense of the term. Owing to the congenitally abstract proclivities of Western thought, the close connection between the practical and the theoretical aspects of Buddhism was gradually ignored, and topics such as the nature of Nirvana came to be discussed as though they had a simply theoretical import that could be determined by the exercise of the speculative reason. The fact that Buddhism is, above all, a way of life was forgotten.

Most of the problems, and many of the misunderstandings, which have arisen in connection with Buddhism, may be traced to this wrong habit of considering the significance of its profoundest teaching in complete dissociation from their pragmatic consequences in the actual Buddhist way of living. Owing to the introduction of a Western-style system of university education, such misunderstandings have taken root, and are flourishing, even here in the soil of India, despite the fact that in this country, even more decidedly than in Greece or Rome, philosophy was traditionally regarded as the theoretical side of religion, and religion as the practical side of philosophy. It therefore becomes necessary to stress the fact that Buddhism is not a system of abstract thought, and that it does not attempt to satisfy mere intellectual curiosity by giving a rationally coherent account of the universe.

Buddhism is a way of life that leads to a spiritual experience; in fact, to a number of experiences. These experiences link up into a series that culminates in the supreme experience of Nirvana. Since it is not only a certain kind of thinking, but also a special way of living, the Dharma of the Enlightened One cannot be adequately understood by the reading of books, even Buddhist books, but only by practising it and making an effort to absorb its spirit into one's life. The teaching of Buddhist philosophy as part of a course of studies the principal aim of which is to 'qualify' the student for secular employment, by professors who make no attempt to put it into practice in their own lives, is really an abuse of Buddhism that will do both teacher and pupil, perhaps, as much harm as good.

Partly by way of a precaution against the danger of regarding Buddhism exclusively from the theoretical point of view, and partly because of the difficulty of giving, briefly, an adequate account of two such vast subjects as Buddhism and art, I propose to elucidate the meaning of Buddhism not by attempting to make a summary of its doctrines, but by endeavouring to present it in a more concrete and poetic manner. The Chinese have a proverb that one illustration is worth a thousand words. I shall seek to make clear the meaning of Buddhism not with one illustration only, but with three. Metaphors, similes, parables, and other literary forms have long been among the recognized vehicles of religious instruction, and owing to their semi-poetic character, they often make a deeper and more enduring impression on our hearts than more learned but more prosaic treatment of the same theme can do.

The following parables, drawn from sources widely separate in time and place, may be considered as illustrating the meaning of Buddhism from what is the most deeply spiritual and, at the same time, the most truly practical standpoint from which it can be viewed.

The first of these may be called the parable of the Well Frog and the Ocean Frog. So well-known to the people of India is this instructive fable that its hero has passed into a proverb, and 'Well Frog' (*kūpa maṇḍūka*) is an expression often applied, not without a touch of humour, to persons of narrow intelligence and bigoted views. The story is given in the words of Swami Vivekananda, by whom it was related, not without effect, at a session of the World's Parliament of Religions held in Chicago on 15 September 1893.

A frog lived in a well. It had lived there for a long time. It was born there and brought up there, and yet was a little, small frog. Of course, the evolutionists were not there then to tell us whether the frog lost its eyes or not, but, for our story's sake, we must take it for granted that it had its eyes, and that it every day cleansed the water of all the worms and bacilli that lived in it with an energy that would do credit to our modern bacteriologists. In this way, it went on and became a little sleek and fat. Well, one day another frog that lived in the sea came and fell into the well.

'Where are you from?'

'I am from the sea.'

'The sea! How big is that? Is it as big as my well?' and he took a leap from one side of the well to the other.

'My friend,' said the frog of the sea, 'how do you compare the sea with your little well?'

Then the frog took another leap and asked, 'Is your sea so big?'

'What nonsense you speak, to compare the sea with your well!'

'Well then,' said the frog in the well, 'nothing can be bigger than my well; there can nothing bigger than this; this fellow is a liar, so turn him out.'[1]

The parable of the Prisoners of the Cave is as permanent a part of the cultural heritage of Europe as that of the Well Frog and the Ocean Frog is of the religious traditions of India. Unlike its popular Eastern parallel, it is not anonymous, but exhibits to a superlative degree that wonderful combination of truth and beauty, of philosophic insight and literary art, for ever associated with the incomparable genius of Plato.

'Imagine a number of men living in an underground cavernous chamber, with an entrance open to the light, extending along the entire length of the cavern, in which they have been confined, from their childhood, with their legs and necks so shackled that they are obliged to sit still and look straight forwards, because their chains render it impossible for them to turn their heads round: and imagine a bright fire burning some way off, above and behind them, and an elevated roadway passing between the fire and the prisoners, with a low wall built along it, like the screens which conjurors put up in front of their audience, and above which they exhibit their wonders.'

'I have it', [Glaucon] replied.

'Also figure to yourself a number of persons walking behind this wall, and carrying with them statues of men, and images of other animals, wrought in wood and stone and all kinds of materials, together with various other articles, which overtop the wall, and, as you might expect, let some of the passers-by be talking and others silent.'

'You are describing a strange scene, and strange prisoners.'

'They resemble us,' I replied. 'For let me ask you, in the first place, whether persons so confined could have seen anything of themselves or of each other, beyond the shadows thrown by the fire upon the part of the cavern facing them?'

'Certainly not, if you suppose them to have been compelled all their lifetime to keep their heads unmoved.'

'And is not their knowledge of the things carried past them equally limited?'

'Unquestionably it is.'

'And if they were able to converse with one another, do you not think that they would be in the habit of giving names to the objects which they saw before them?'

'Doubtless they would.'

'Again, if their prison-house returned an echo from the part facing them, whenever one of the passers-by opened his lips, to what, let me ask you, could they refer the voice, if not to the shadow which was passing?'

'Unquestionably they would refer it to that.'

'Then surely such persons would hold the shadows of those manufactured articles to be the only realities.'

'Without a doubt they would.'

'Now consider what would happen if the course of nature brought them a release from their fetters, and a remedy for their foolishness, in the following manner. Let us suppose that one of them has been released, and compelled suddenly to stand up, and turn his neck round and walk with open eyes towards the light and let us suppose that he goes through all these actions with pain, and that the dazzling splendour renders him incapable of discerning those objects of which he used formerly to see the shadows. What answer should you expect him to make, if some one were to tell him that in those days he was watching foolish phantoms, but that now he is somewhat nearer to reality, and is turned towards things more real, and sees more correctly; above all, if he were to point out to him the several objects that are passing by, and question him, and compel him to answer what they are? Should you not expect him to be puzzled, and to regard his old visions as truer than the objects now forced upon his notice?'

'Yes, much truer.'

'And if he were further compelled to gaze at the light itself, would not his eyes, think you, be distressed, and would he not shrink and turn away to the things which he could see distinctly, and consider them to be really clearer than the things pointed out to him?'

'Just so.'

'And if some one were to drag him violently up the rough and steep ascent from the cavern, and refuse to let him go till he had drawn him out into the light of the sun, would he not, think you, be vexed and indignant at such treatment, and on reaching the light, would he not find his eyes so dazzled by the glare as to be incapable of making out so much as one of the objects which are now called true?'

'Yes, he would find it so at first.'[2]

Such is the tremendous myth which Plato puts into the mouth of Socrates at the beginning of the seventh book of *The Republic*.

Our third and last parable carries us from Greece to India; from the house of Polemarchus in the Piraeus, outside Athens, to the Jeta Grove, in Anathapindika's Park near Savatthi; from the noise and excitement of the Thracian festival in the fifth century BCE, back to the quarrels and disputations of recluses and Brahmanas in the sixth. So serious had these quarrels and disputes at one time become that they attracted the attention of certain bhikkhus, who came to the Buddha and reported the matter to Him. After condemning the behaviour of those sectarians in strong terms, the Buddha related the parable of the Blind Men and the Elephant. This parable was subsequently included in the repertoire of Indian storytellers, and appears frequently in popular religious literature. By a strange twist of interpretation, however, it is now quoted as an illustration of the belief that all religions are equally true. An examination of the Buddha's own words will reveal the fallaciousness of such an interpretation.

'Now in former times, brethren, there was a rajah in this same Savatthi. Then, brethren, that rajah called to a certain man, saying, "Come thou, good fellow! Go and gather together all the blind men that are in Savatthi!"

"Very good, your majesty", replied that man, and in obedience to the rajah gathered together all the blind men, took them with him to the rajah and said, "Your majesty, all the blind men of Savatthi are now assembled."

"Then, my good man, show these blind men an elephant."

"Very good, your majesty", said the man, and did as he was told, saying, "O ye blind, such as this is an elephant!"

'And to one he presented the head of the elephant, to another the ear, to another a tusk, the trunk, the foot, back, tail, and tuft of the tail, saying to each one that it was the elephant.

'Now, brethren, that man having presented the elephant to the blind men, came to the rajah and said, "Your majesty, the elephant has been presented to the blind men. Do what is your will."

'Thereupon, brethren, that rajah went up to the blind men and said to each, "Have you studied the elephant?"

' "Yes, your majesty."

' "Then tell me your conclusions about him."

'Thereupon those who had been presented with the head answered, "Your majesty, an elephant is just like a pot." And those who had only observed the ear replied, "An elephant is just like a winnowing basket." Those who had been presented with the tusk said it was a ploughshare. Those who knew only the trunk said it was a plough. "The body", said they, "is a granary: the foot, a pillar: the back, a mortar: its tail, a pestle: the tuft of the tail, just a besom." Then they began to quarrel, shouting, "Yes it is! No it isn't! An elephant is not that! Yes, it's like that:" and so on, till they came to fisticuffs about the matter.

'Then, brethren, that rajah was delighted with the scene.

'Just so are these sectarians, who are wanderers, blind, unseeing, knowing not the truth, but each maintaining that "it is thus and thus." '

Whereupon the Exalted One on that occasion, seeing the gist of the matter, uttered this solemn saying:

'O how they cling and wrangle, some who claim
Of brahmin and recluse the honoured name.
For quarrelling, each to his view, they cling.
Such folk see only one side of a thing.'[3]

These three parables illustrate different aspects of one truth. Each of them contains two different characters, or sets of characters, one representing a wider, more illumined, and more comprehensive state of consciousness; the other, a state of mind comparatively narrow, unillumined, and exclusive. In the first parable, the parochial outlook of the Well Frog, who dwells within a limited range of consciousness, represented by the waters of the well, is sharply contrasted with the ampler vision of his visitor, the Ocean Frog, who inhabits a realm of consciousness which is infinite. Between those who, in the parable of the Prisoners of the Cave, are still fettered and can perceive only shadows flitting across the rear wall of their prison, and the released prisoner who has been dragged out of the cave and compelled to behold the light of day, a similar difference may be observed. The third parable contrasts the correct idea of an elephant possessed by a man of normal sight with the erroneous notions entertained by the blind, thus illustrating the enormous discrepancy between the all-embracing wisdom of the Buddha and the one-sided opinions of the sectarian teachers of His time. Thus we have, on the one hand, an infinite consciousness, represented by the waters of the ocean, the light of day, and the eyesight of a healthy man, and on the other, a narrow state of consciousness illustrated by the waters of the well, the gloom of the cave, and the eyesight of the blind.

This difference renders possible two movements in consciousness, a movement of expansion from a narrower to a wider state, and a diametrically opposite movement of contraction from a wider to a narrower state.

Buddhism, as a way of life, as a practicable scheme of spiritual development, is based on the first movement, the movement of expansion. It aims at lifting us out of the well and plunging us into the ocean; at leading us from the darkness of the cave into the glorious light of the sun; at healing us of our spiritual blindness and restoring to our eyes the divine vision that they have lost. Ethically speaking this expansive movement in consciousness consists in a continual renunciation of the self, in a constant progression from egoism to selflessness. Though twenty-five centuries of history have led Buddhism to many new developments, particularly in the field of spiritual practice and meditational technique, the validity of such developments is to be tested by this criterion. If they lead to an expansion of consciousness, to an illumination of mind and purification of heart, to a higher degree of spiritual sharpsightedness, to emancipation from the fetters of egoism, then they may be considered as the teaching of the Master Himself. The Buddha stands alone among the founders of religions in not merely permitting, but even demanding, that instead of accepting His words on trust, we should believe them only after having verified their truth in our own spiritual experience, testing them, in His own expressive simile, as on the touchstone the goldsmith tests his gold.

Our spatial metaphor may be elaborated, and the meaning of Buddhism rendered still more explicit, by pointing out that expansion takes place in two planes, the vertical and the horizontal. By an upward or downward movement of expansion in consciousness is meant a heightening or deepening (the two expressions come to much the same thing) of experience, an increase of insight, or augmentation of understanding; by a movement of expansion outwards is meant a constant multiplication of our points of contact with the external world, a ceaseless enlargement and elaboration of that delicate network of sympathy and affection by which we are connected in a thousand ways not only with all other human beings, but with every other form of life. To the upward and downward movement of expansion in consciousness, Buddhism gives the name 'wisdom' (*prajñā*); the movement of expansion outwards, it terms 'compassion' (*karuṇā*). We shall not greatly err if, from a strictly practical and spiritual point of view, we find in a life dedicated to the expansion of consciousness through the development of wisdom and compassion the ultimate meaning of Buddhism.

Having made the meaning of Buddhism clear at least for practical purposes, we must now investigate its relation to art. By art is not meant, as people so often suppose, merely the art of painting, but the sister arts of music and poetry, architecture and sculpture, as well. That Buddhism is justly famous not only for the richness and beauty of its artistic flowerings in India, but also for the fertility and vigour of the seeds it scattered all over Asia, is a commonplace of the history of oriental art that need not be repeated here. What we propose to trace, however, is not the relation between Buddhism and art on the historical level, but their connection on the immeasurably deeper levels of psychology and the spiritual life. We do not intend to trace the vicissitudes of Buddhist themes as the subject-matter of art, or to give either a description or a critical account of Buddhist painting, sculpture, architecture, or literature, but simply to ascertain the nature of the inner connection, as two independent branches of human experience, between Buddhism as Buddhism and art as art. For only then shall we be able to estimate the value of art from the spiritual point of view.

Neither the relation of art to Buddhism nor its spiritual value can, however, be determined, until we have first acquainted ourselves with the precise nature of the subject of our inquiry. The word 'art', like all other general ideas, is a mere abstraction, and no more denotes an actually existing object than the words 'liberty', 'freedom', 'independence', and similar terms of which newspapers make such lavish use, denote concrete things existing either in the world of facts or in the realm of ideas. There is no such thing as art. Only works of art exist. No investigation into the nature of art can be fruitful that does not begin and end with a consideration of the nature of concrete pictures and poems.

Back to earth, then, we come from the cloudy heavens of abstraction and proceed to plant our feet firmly on the ground with an analysis of the individual art-work into its two component parts. These parts may be described, if a not too exact usage of scholastic terminology be permitted us, as substance and as form. By the substance of a work of art we mean the degree of sensitiveness or sensibility, the state of consciousness, the kind of experience or realization, which it expresses and communicates. Form, on the other hand, is the pleasurable pattern of sensations into which the rarified thoughts and emotions of the artist condense and crystallize themselves and through which they find embodiment and expression. A refinement of analysis may help to define the second part more clearly. Even as the work of art is divisible into substance and form, so is the form in turn susceptible of a further division into a sensuous content and an organization of that sensuous content by means of pattern and rhythm. Eye and ear being the most prominent of the organs of sense, it follows that sensations of colour and shape (really we should telescope the words and say 'colourshape', as the two 'things', though distinguishable, are inseparable), and sensations of sound, provide the artist with the raw material of his creations. Brooding upon the chaos of visual sensations, the spirit of the artist begets dove-like the cosmos of painting, sculpture, and architecture; spreading wings over the abyss of sound, it produces the universe of poetry and music. At the fiat of creative genius the discordant atoms of sensation 'in order to their stations leap', and obey, not the power of music, but the power whence music itself derives its influence.

Through their organization of visual sensations by means of the harmonious arrangement of colours, shapes, and surfaces, and of auditory sensations by means of rhythm and melody, the painter, the sculptor, and the architect, on the one hand, and the poet and the musician, on the other, make patterns that are beautiful and which produce pleasure. These pleasurable patterns of sensations, which compose the form of a work of art, are in turn arranged in such a way as to express the artist's feelings and sense of values, which make up what we have termed its substance.

Without entering into the psychology of artistic creation, or attempting to investigate the nature of that mysterious urge by which his life is dominated and sometimes destroyed, it may be affirmed that, from the viewpoint of the artist, there is a movement from substance to form, from the feelings that arise so irresistibly within him and the ultimate embodiment of those feelings in metal, wood, and stone, in pigment, words, and notes. This movement is creation. From the viewpoint of one who reads a poem, looks at a picture, or listens to a song, there is a movement from form to substance, from patterns made of certain visual and auditory sensations, from patches of colour and snatches of sound, to participation in the experience they embody. This movement is one of enjoyment or appreciation. But whether, in respect of the creative and appreciative experience of a work of art, there takes place a movement from substance to form, or from form to substance, it is of far greater importance to our present inquiry that there occurs in both cases that stretching of the mind 'some distance beyond the limits of the understanding', which Herbert Read has clearly recognized as 'the function of art',[4] and which we have already discovered and described, in the form of an expansion of consciousness, as constituting the spiritual meaning of Buddhism. In the case of the artist, the stretching or expansion is the cause of which the work of art is the effect. In the case of the enjoyer or appreciator (we would use the less clumsy appellation 'critic', if it had not acquired such an unsympathetic connotation), the stretching of the mind beyond the limits of understanding, or the expansion of consciousness beyond the boundaries of selfhood, is the effect whereof the work of art is the cause.

As with the expansion of consciousness through Buddhism, so, with its expansion by means of art, the movement of expansion takes place in two directions, on two planes. In Buddhism there is a movement of wisdom upwards or downwards, and a movement of compassion outwards. Corresponding to this, there is in art an intensification or heightening of sensibility, as well as an extension or widening of sympathy. Some forms of art have a tendency to expand our consciousness in one direction rather than in another, while others expand it in both. Lyric poetry, for instance, lifts our gross human emotions of love and anguish, hope and despair, to so high a pitch of intensity that earthly passions are refined into spiritual raptures, and our whole emotional being keyed to a higher and purer octave of feeling. Classical music, whether Eastern or Western, often produces the same kind of effect. Dramatic poetry, on the contrary, by introducing us to men and women of every imaginable age and country, with every conceivable variation of character and circumstances; by compelling us to watch with interest and concern the vicissitudes of their fortunes; by forcing us to weep with them in their day of sorrow, and rejoice with them in their hour of mirth, extends and enlarges the house of our sympathies by a thousand ramifications into the many mansions of other lives. Epic and narrative poetry generally stretch the mind in the same direction as the dramatic; and so, on a lower level, do the novel and the short story.

Such a distribution of functions between the fine arts

should not, however, be taken in too literal and exclusive a sense, or regarded as being of very great importance to our present inquiry. All that we now wish to insist upon is the fact that every genuine work of art enlarges the circle of our consciousness, and that in this enlargement of consciousness the value of a work of art, from the spiritual point of view, consists.

Just as there are two kinds of expansion of consciousness, so within each kind are there infinite degrees of expansion. Some works of art lift us, as it were, only a few inches above the ground; others transport us to the empyrean. This difference of degree, whereby we distinguish the palpitations of Tom Moore from the authentic thrill of Shelley, is due to a difference in the quality of their inspiration. It is one of the great merits of Sri Aurobindo's literary criticism that he so clearly distinguishes the different levels whence the flow of poetic inspiration may descend. Without necessarily endorsing all the details of his stratification of existence, we can both recognize and make use of the truth enunciated in the following passage.

> As for the originating source of poetry, it may be anywhere, the subtle physical plane, the higher or lower vital itself, the dynamic or creative intelligence, the plane of dynamic vision, the psychic, the illumined mind— even, though this is the rarest, the overmind. To get the overmind inspiration through is so rare that there are only a few lines or short passages in all poetic literature that give at least some appearance or reflection of it.[5]

Coupling Sri Aurobindo's doctrine with our own discovery, we may say that the higher the source of artistic inspiration the greater is the expansion of consciousness involved and the higher the spiritual value of the work of art produced. Care should be taken, though, not to confuse the essentially spiritual function of art as *art* with the didacticism of conventionally religious art. To make the matter clearer, it will be convenient to summarize a classification which we have made elsewhere.

From the dual viewpoint of subject matter and quality of inspiration, four categories of art can be distinguished. The first is neither religious in form nor spiritualizing in effect. Spawned as it is in the slimiest depths of our psychic nature, it not only fails to expand our consciousness, but, pandering to our lust for sex and crime, thrusts us down into the hell of an even lower and narrower range of consciousness. In modern life examples of this kind of art are legion, and specification would be almost invidious. Tabloid newspapers, pulp magazines, and the majority of popular films may be mentioned as the principal purveyors of this pseudo-artistic trash. The second category of art is that which is formally, but not essentially, religious. Such are the lithographed pictures of gods and saints and religious teachers which one finds in the possession of devout people all over the world. Though religious in theme, they are either technically inept or executed in mechanical fashion, without feeling, and do not produce an expansion of consciousness so much as condition a devotional reflex. Thirdly, we have a type of art that is essentially, though not formally, religious. Chinese landscape painting springs at once to mind as the almost classic example of this category of art. Though devoid of any formally religious content, such paintings are in the deepest sense spiritual. The extraordinary sense of liberation and infinite expansion of consciousness that they produce in the spectator being sufficient proof of the tremendous height of inspiration whence, like a cataract that 'smokes upon the mountain-side', they descend through brushes and black ink onto rolls of silk.

The fourth and last of our categories includes works of art that are both formally and essentially religious. Enough has been said of the three previous categories to make clear, without need of further explanation, the nature of this one, the crown and flower of them all. The ancient Buddhist art of India and Ceylon, China and Japan, Tibet and Cambodia, may without reproach of partiality be allowed the honour of representing this supreme class. Though it is difficult, even impossible, to single out any one type of Buddhist art as being more typical of the whole group than are others, it will no doubt be conceded that the sedent image of the Buddha in meditation is the most popular and widely known of all. Here the meaning of Buddhism and the value of art coalesce upon the lips of the Buddha into a smile that expresses what is, perhaps, the greatest expansion of consciousness that it is possible for the plastic arts to meditate.

From how high a quality of inspiration the work of art issued, we hardly dare to guess. How tremendous an effect it can have upon the whole character may be understood from a story which we heard a few weeks ago from a French lady, a scholar in Sanskrit and poetess in her own language, now a Buddhist nun in India, who had received so deep an impression—a spiritual shock of such high voltage—from an image of this kind which she had seen in the Musee Guimet in Paris, that she resolved to consecrate her whole life to the study and practice of Buddhism, so as to experience for herself, to however small an extent, that liberation of consciousness, that wisdom and compassion, which shone through those stone features as though they had been transparent to a light within.

An archaic torso of Apollo that the poet Rilke saw in a museum seems to have produced a similar transformation in his consciousness; but since he was a poet, the transformation was not so much reflected in his life as registered in his art. Not that he was unaware of the spiritual significance of deep aesthetic experience. He was, perhaps, more conscious of the inner relations between the experience of the saint and the experience of the artist than any modern poet, and this consciousness makes him, in an age when external contact between religion and art has been broken off, an artist whose work is of very special significance and value. If the first thirteen and a half lines of his sonnet, *An Archaic Torso of Apollo*, show how deep, how heartfelt, was his experience of beauty, the concluding one and a half lines, which mark an abrupt, almost a violent, transition from the descriptive to the reflective mood, reveal how clearly he understood the ethical and spiritual demands of that experience, and how little afraid he was to meet and grapple with them. His meaning is unmistakable, as feeling abruptly deepens into insight and he cries out

Here is no place
That does not see you. You must change your life.

This change of life, this transformation of character and attitude, constitutes not only the message of the Buddha image and of the archaic torso of Apollo, but, as we have tried to show, the essence and meaning of Buddhism and the real value of art as well.

Buddhism and art both effect a two-dimensional expansion in consciousness, the practical results that they achieve are of the same kind, however greatly such results may vary in degree, and however dissimilar may be the methods employed by Buddhism, on the one hand, and art, on the other, to bring them about. Buddhism effects an expansion of consciousness by acting directly on the understanding and the will: art produces a change of life indirectly, by appealing to our sense of beauty. Since man possesses an emotional as well as an intellectual and a volitional nature, and is capable of response to beauty no less than to truth and goodness, it is necessary for him to develop and expand simultaneously the emotional, intellectual, and volitional aspects of his personality. Buddhism and art, therefore, are both indispensable to a balanced spiritual life. Not that we intend to suggest an absolutely exclusive distribution of functions between them, allotting to Buddhism the sole responsibility for developing the mind, and to art the sole responsibility for developing the emotions. Every thought possesses emotional colouring, however obscure. Buddhism, though acting primarily on the intellect, certainly makes a powerful secondary appeal to the emotions, especially to the devotional feelings, which are developed as fully, though not so one-sidedly, in members of the Buddhist community as in people belonging to religions that appeal more to the heart than to the head, to faith rather than to reason. Art, though it operates on the imagination directly, does not fail to influence the understanding. In poetry especially, it is impossible to dissociate the emotional impact of a work of art from the framework of objective reference to which it is attached and which constitutes its 'meaning' for the intellect.

Whether the life of any particular person will be dominated more by interests pertaining to Buddhism, or more by interests pertaining to art, is a question that will be determined by the relative strength in him of reason and of emotion. We are concerned only to insist, first of all that the meaning of Buddhism coincides with the value of art; and secondly, that the development of understanding and insight through the one, and of imagination and sensitiveness to beauty through the other is, for modern men and women, in whom the emotional life and the intellectual life are of almost equal vividness and vigour, not only a need, but almost a necessity.

Despite the obviously spiritualizing influence of many great works of art, there may be found, in different communities and religious bodies, people who think that religion and art are mutually exclusive, and that one who takes his religious life seriously ought to have no more to do with art than with drinking, dancing, and gambling. Puritans of this brand believe that since art makes its appeal through the senses—through eye and ear—its content is necessarily sensual and even sexual. To their way of thinking, which is wholly incapable of visualizing the wider horizons into which a life of genuine spirituality may open, an artistic life is practically synonymous with a career of immorality.

Whenever a reaction against puritanism sets in, its supporters generally go to the other extreme and proclaim the doctrine of art for art's sake. The middle way between these two extreme views is indicated by Sri Aurobindo, who in some published letters to his poet-disciples has advanced what appears to be a satisfactory solution of the problem. All four extracts given below have been taken from Section Eight (dealing with *Poetic Creation and Yoga* and with *Utility of Literature, etc. in Sādhana*) of the Third Series of his letters, to which those interested in the subject are referred for further information.

> (i) A literary man is one who loves literature and literary activities for their own separate sake. A Yogi who writes is not a literary man, for he writes only what the inner Will and Word wants him to express. He is a channel and instrument of something greater than his own literary personality.[6]
>
> (ii) I have always told you that you ought not to stop your poetry and similar activities. It is a mistake to do so out of asceticism or *tapasya.* One can stop these things when they drop of themselves, because one is full of experience and so interested in one's inner life that one has no energy to spare for the rest. Even then, there is no rule for giving up, for there is no reason why poetry etc. should not be a part of *Sādhana*[7].
>
> (iii) It would be a mistake to silence the poetic flow on

principle; the creative habit is a tonic to the vital and keeps it in a good condition, and the practice of *sādhana* needs a strong and widening vital for its support. There is not real incompatibility between the creative power and silence; for the real silence is something inward, and it does not or at least need not cease when a strong activity or expression rises to the surface.[8]

(iv) The Vedic poets regarded the poetry as *mantras*, they were the vehicles of their own realizations for others. . . Anything that carries the Word, the Light in it, spoken or written, can light this fire within, open a sky, as it were, being the effective vision of which the Word is the body. . . In all ages spiritual seekers have expressed their aspirations or their experiences in poetry or inspired language, and it has helped them and others. Therefore, there is nothing absurd in my assigning to such poetry a spiritual or psychic value and effectiveness of a psychic or spiritual character.[9]

This firm and emphatic vindication of the spiritual function of poetry, and, by implication, of the arts in general, could hardly be bettered, and may be allowed to stand as an adequate reply to all the objections which puritanism may urge against the creation and enjoyment of works of art.

But one serious difficulty still remains to be faced. Granting that the inner relation between Buddhism and art is such as we have described, and that art is, or at least can be, as Sri Aurobindo maintains, 'a part of *sādhana*', are we justified in assuming that such a view of the matter is correct from the standpoint of orthodox Buddhism? Are we not guilty of misrepresenting the Buddhist doctrine of the value of art? Buddhist art is undoubtedly a glorious achievement from the artistic point of view. But can it be regarded as a strictly Buddhist achievement? Is it not rather a beautiful excrescence on the trunk of Buddhism, like the mistletoe on the oak, or the orchid on the elm?

Some Buddhists do, in fact, seem to be of this opinion. They believe that the arts stimulate sexual desire, and that the Buddha, therefore, prohibited his bhikkhu disciples from enjoying works of art. For them this prohibition is implicit in the Eighth Precept, observed by all bhikkhus, and by lay devotees on the *uposatha* days: *Nacca-gīta-vādita-visūkha-dassana veramaṇī sikkhāpadaṁ samādiyāmi*[10], which is generally translated as 'I observe the precept of abstaining from dances, songs, instrumental music, and theatrical performances.' This precept, they maintain, in effect excludes not only the enjoyment of the arts of singing, dancing, and music, but also of poetry and painting, sculpture and architecture, from all of which a true follower of the Buddha should hold himself rigidly aloof. Buddhism is, in their opinion, puritanical in its attitude to art. An enlightened mind, which is free from even the slightest taint of desire, is by its very nature incapable of aesthetic enjoyment, for such enjoyment, they believe, is of a fundamentally sensuous and even sexual character.

Whether Buddhism agrees with this puritanical evaluation of the nature and function of art, or whether its view of the relation between the spiritual life and the artistic life approximates to that which we have taken above, is a question which can be answered firstly by referring to Sri Aurobindo's teaching about the different levels, from the subtle physical to that of the Overmind, whence artistic inspiration can originate, and secondly by an appeal to the personal example of the Buddha.

From information available in the Three Baskets (*Tipiṭaka*) of canonical scriptures, and in their commentaries, it is evident that the dancing, singing, instrumental music, and theatrical performances of the Eighth Precept belonged to the first of our four categories of art, that is to say, they were neither religious in form nor spiritualizing in effect. Like the songs, dances, and orchestral music of the contemporary film, they originated from what Sri Aurobindo terms the subtle physical and vital planes, and it may be contended that the Buddha required His disciples to abstain from such kinds of entertainment not because they were art, but because they were not art of that deeper and more genuine kind which we have included in the third and fourth of our categories. The prohibitions of the Eighth Precept can no more be generalized into a total exclusion of all kinds of art from the purview of the spiritual life than, for example, a contemporary spiritual master's disapproval of cinema-going could be construed as a condemnation of classical music, or of poetry and painting. Sri Aurobindo, whose views on the spiritual function of art we have quoted so extensively, says of novel-reading in *sādhana*: 'If novels touch the lower vital or raise it, they ought not be read by the *sādhaka*.'[11] No contradiction is involved in prohibiting one kind of art to the spiritual aspirant and permitting him the other. Indeed, it is just what might have been expected.

But even though, in imparting the Eighth Precept to His monastic disciples and lay devotees, the Buddha intended no more than a prohibition of the ancient Indian equivalent of dance-music, what evidence is there (it may be demanded) that He regarded the appreciation of art, the enjoyment and creation of painting, poetry, and music, as being compatible with the demands of the spiritual life? If the records of His life and teaching contain even one reference to His appreciation of the beauties of art, it will be sufficient to prove that such appreciation is not impossible to the enlightened mind and that, therefore, the content of art is compatible with the content of spirituality. We shall cite not merely one but three such references, the first demonstrating His appreciation of music, the second His approval of poetry, and the third His sensitiveness to visual beauty.

The Buddha's appreciation of music is recorded in the

Sakka-pañha Suttanta of the *Dīgha Nikāya*, the first of the five great divisions of the *Sutta Piṭaka* or 'Basket of Discourses'. Sakka, king of the gods, wished to ask the Buddha certain questions; but seeing that He was absorbed in meditation hesitated to approach Him. He, therefore, sent in advance one of the *gandharvas*, or celestial musicians, of his court, whose skill in music and song is in Indian literature as famous, though not as fatal, as that of the Sirens in the literature of the West. We quote the whole of this charming episode, which provides an introduction of great literary beauty to the more serious discussions between the Buddha and Sakka which make up the bulk of this Suttanta.

> Then said Sakka, the king of the gods, to Five-crest, the *gandhabba*: 'Difficult of approach, dear Five-crest, are the Tathagatas, to one like me, when they are rapt in the bliss of meditation, and for that purpose abiding in solitude. But if you were first to gain over the Exalted One [by your music], then might I afterwards come up and visit him, the Arahant, the Buddha supreme.'
>
> 'So be it and good luck to you!' consented Five-crest, and taking his lyre he went to the Indra-sal-tree-cave. On coming there he thought: 'Thus far will the Exalted One be neither too far from me nor too near to me, and He will hear my voice.' And he stood on one side, and let his lyre be heard and recited these verses concerning the Awakened One and the Truth, the Arahants and Love:
>
> *Lady, thy father Timbaru I greet*
> *With honour due, O Glory-of-the-Sun!*
> *In that he wrought a thing so nobly fair*
> *As thou, O fount divine of all my joy!*

Sweet as the breeze to one foredone with sweat,
Sweet as a cooling drink to one athirst,
So dear art thou, O presence radiant!
To me, dear as to Arahants the Truth.

As medicine bringing ease to one that's sick,
As food to starving man, so, Lady, quench,
As with cool waters, me who am all aflame.

E'en as an elephant, fretted by hook,
Dashes unheeding curb and goad aside,
So I, crazed by the beauty of thy form,
Know not the why and wherefore of my acts.

By thee my heart is held in bonds and all
Bent out of course: nor can I turn me back,
No more than fish, once he hath ta'en the bait.

Within thine arm embrace me, lady, me
With thy soft languid eyne embrace and hold,
O nobly fair! This I entreat of thee.

Scanty in sooth, O maid of waving locks,
Was my desire, but now it swelleth aye,
Indefinitely great, e'en as the gifts
Made by the faithful to the Arahants.

Whate'er of merit to such holy ones
I've wrought, be thou, O altogether fair,
Be thou the fruit thereof to fall to me.

Whate'er of other merit I have wrought
In the wide world, O altogether fair,
Be thou the fruit thereof to fall to me.

As the great Sakyan Seer, through ecstacy
Rapt and intent and self-possessed, doth brood
Seeking ambrosia, even so do I
Pursue the quest of thee, O Glory-of-the-Sun!

As would that Seer rejoice, were he to win
Ineffable Enlightenment, so I
With thee made one, O fairest, were in bliss.

And if perchance a boon were granted me
By Sakka, lord of Three-and-Thirty gods,
'Tis Thee I'd ask of him, lady, so strong

My love. And for thy father, wisest maid—
Him as a Sal-tree freshly burgeoning
I worship for such peerless offspring given.

When Five-crest had finished, the Exalted One said to him: 'The sound of your strings, Five-crest, so harmonizes with that of your song, and the sound of your voice with that of the strings, that your lyre does not too much colour your song, nor your song too much colour your play. Where, Five-crest, did you learn these verses "concerning the Awakened One and the Truth, the Arahants and Love?"

'The Exalted One, lord, was once staying at Uruvela, on the bank of the Neranjara river, at the foot of the Goat-herd's Banyan tree before He attained to Enlightenment. Now at that time, lord, the lady called Bhadda, in appearance as Sunshine, daughter of Timbaru, king of the *gandhabbas*, was beloved by me. But that lady, lord, was in love with another, Sikhaddi, son of Matali, the charioteer. And since I could not get the lady by any method whatever, I took my lyre of yellow Beluva wood, and going to the abode of Timbaru, king of the *gandhabbas*, I played my lyre and recited these verses "concerning the Awakened One and the Truth, the Arahants and Love" [the text here repeats the verses].

'And when I had finished, lord, the lady Suriyavaccasa said to me: "That Blessed One, sir, I have not seen face to face, and yet I heard of Him when I went to dance at the Sudhamma Hall of the Three-and-Thirty gods. Since you extol the Blessed One, let there be a meeting between thee and me today." So, lord, I met that lady, not on that day but afterwards.'[12]

At the end of the *Suttanta* Sakka, the king of the gods, having obtained from the Buddha satisfactory answers to all his questions, and having gained 'the stainless spotless Eye for the Truth', in return for the services he had rendered made Five-crest king of the *gandhabbas* and bestowed upon him the hand of the lady Suriyavaccasa. This idyllic episode reveals not only the Buddha's appreciation of music, but also His tender humanity. One can almost imagine the smile of amusement with which the Passionless One listened to the woes of the love-lorn *gandhabba*.

The Buddha's appreciation of poetry has been recorded in the *Vangīsa Saṁyutta*, the Eighth Section of the *Saṁyutta Nikāya* (Book of the Kindred Sayings). Vangisa was one of the most gifted of the Buddha's disciples, and each of the group of twelve suttas bearing his name contains a piece of poetry together with a prose introduction narrating the circumstances that led to its composition. The poetry is included, without the prose, in the *Thera-gāthā*, or 'Songs of the Elder Bhikkhus', one of the books of the *Khuddaka Nikāya,* which also contains verses by Vangisa from the *Sutta Nipāta* not found in the *Saṁyutta*. The first four poems are verses of self-condemnation, of repentance for lust and pride, and express the poet's determination to attain to the extinction of all mental impurities in the passionless peace of *nibbana*. The following seven suttas, most of which contain verses of great literary beauty, reveal the Buddha and, in one case, Sariputta also as encouraging Vangisa in the exercise of his poetic gift.

Sutta XI is short and poetic enough to be quoted in full as a typical example of the Buddha's attitude.

> The Exalted One was once staying at Campa, on the shore of the Lotus-pool, at Gaggara. And with Him was a great company of brethren, even five hundred, and seven hundred lay adherents, and seven hundred lay women adherents, and some thousands of *devas*. Among them all of a truth the Exalted One shone exceedingly in beauty and in glory.
>
> Then the venerable Vangisa, arising from his seat, and draping his outer robe over one shoulder, bent his clasped hands saluting towards the Exalted One, and said: 'It is revealed to me, Exalted One! It is revealed to me, Blessed One!'
>
> And the Exalted One said: 'Be it revealed to thee, Vangisa.'
>
> Then the venerable Vangisa extolled the Exalted One in His presence with appropriate verses:
>
> *As when the clouds have drifted from the sky*
> *The moon shines as a sun immaculate,*
> *So thou, Angirasa, great seer, yet more*
> *Dost gloriously the world illuminate.'*[13]

In each of the other six suttas, also, Vangisa is encouraged to make use of his by no means inconsiderable poetic talents, and he improvises verses on 'speech that is well spoken', in praise of Sariputta, on occasion of the *pavāraṇā* ceremony, on the preaching of the Buddha, on Annasi-Kondanna's homage to the Master, and in recognition of the psychic power of Moggallana. Sutta VIII contains not only the permission to improvise for which Vangisa asks, and the Buddha invariably grants, but a few additional lines of dialogue, not found in the other suttas, which prove how emphatic was the Blessed

One's approval, and how unambiguous His encouragement, of the type of poetry in which Vangisa excelled. After Vangisa, in a burst of enthusiasm, had compared the Buddha preaching the Dharma to His disciples to a great storm-cloud pouring down plenteous rain upon the earth and had concluded with a stanza in adoration of the Master, the Exalted One said:

> 'Say now, Vangisa, were these verses thought out by thee beforehand, or have they been revealed to thee just on the spot?'
>
> 'Nay, lord, these verses were not thought out by me beforehand: they were revealed to me just on the spot.'
>
> 'Wherefore, Vangisa, let yet more verses, not thought out beforehand, be revealed to thee just on the spot.'
>
> 'So be it, lord' replied Vangisa, and in additional verses not thought out beforehand he extolled the Exalted One:
>
> *O'er Mara's devious ways faring triumphant,*
> *Thou breakest up the fallows of our hearts.*
> *Behold Him from all bondage our deliverer,*
> *Himself full fraught the harvest he imparts.*
>
> *Yea, Thou hast shown a Way by many methods*
> *For crossing o'er the torrent safe to land;*
> *And that Ambrosial thus manifested,*
> *Norm-seers inexpugnable we stand.*
>
> *Light-bringer, He hath pierced beyond, beholding*
> *Past all those stations [where we end our flight],*
> *The topmost height knowing and realizing,*
> *He showeth us that vantage-point of sight.*

Lo! Now in truth so well revealed, for trifling
What place is there for those who learn His Lore?
Hence zealously within that Master's system
Train ye alway, and while ye train adore.'[14]

In the sixth century BCE Indian painting had not yet embarked upon the career which was to culminate in the frescoes that glorify the caves of Ajanta, and we are, therefore, precluded from referring to any instance of the Buddha's appreciation of visual art in its more refined and developed forms. At least one example, however, can be cited of His sensitiveness to the beauty of the human body in motion, and to the harmonious effect of contrasted colours; and, inasmuch as form and colour constitute the two basic elements of the visual arts, the Buddha's appreciation of them as they occur in nature may be understood as being in principle not different from the appreciation of the arts of painting and sculpture. Our example is taken from the *Mahāparinibbāna Suttanta* of the *Dīgha Nikāya,* which is admitted to contain some of the oldest and most authentic material found in the Pali canon. The passage throws an interesting sidelight on contemporary sartorial fashions.

> Now the Licchavis of Vesali heard that the Exalted One had arrived in Vesali, and was staying at Ambapali's grove. And ordering a number of state carriages to be made ready, they each mounted one of them and went forth with their train from Vesali. Some of them were dark, dark in colour, and wearing dark clothes and ornaments: some of them were fair, fair in colour, and wearing light clothes and ornaments: some of them were red, ruddy in colour, and wearing red clothes and ornaments: some of them were white, pale in colour, and wearing white clothes and ornaments.
>
> When the Exalted One saw the Licchavis approaching in

the distance, He addressed the brethren and said: 'O brethren, let those of the brethren who have never seen the Tavatimsa gods, gaze upon this company of the Licchavis, behold this company of the Licchavis, compare this company of the Licchavis— for they are even as a company of Tavatimsa gods.'[15]

The simile implied by this passage is not present by an accident. Aesthetic emotion naturally tends to express itself, on the literary side, in figures of speech of various kinds. That the Buddha, moved by the beauty of the richly dressed and ornamented Licchavis, should have compared them to a company of celestial beings, is not attributable to any desire on his part for the edification of the brethren, but rather to the spontaneous outburst of His aesthetic emotions.

In addition to these specific instances of the Buddha's own appreciation of art, it is possible to adduce in support of our contention that, even from the orthodox Buddhist point of view, the content of art is not incompatible with the content of spirituality, and that the religious life does not exclude artistic interests, a number of general considerations. Since the Buddha's teachings were preserved not by means of pictures of musical notation, but in words that were subsequently written down in books as works of literature, it is inevitable that these considerations should be of a predominantly literary character. One of the first things that arrest our attention when we take up any canonical Pali book is that a great deal of it is in verse. Some books, indeed, such as the *Dhammapada* and the *Sutta Nipāta*, consist either entirely of verses, or contain only a small intermixture of prose passages. The *Thera-* and *Theri- gāthās* or Psalms of the Elder Brethren and Elder Sisters, many of them extemporized after their composer's enlightenment, are, perhaps, the most outstanding examples of the former class. Besides being spiritual documents of rare value, they contain gems of spiritual poetry of the highest water, and Mrs Rhys Davids, in the Introduction to her pioneer work of translation, Psalms of the Early Buddhists—I: The Brethren, has not hesitated to compare the most poetically gifted of the *theras* with Keats and Shelley. Though felicity of verbal music is the basis of her comparison, it is by no means the only point of similarity between the verses of the Indian and English poets. Like the Romantics, the *theras* had an eye for the beauties of nature, and Mrs Rhys Davids goes so far as to suggest—the idea might shock an 'orthodox' Buddhist—that they sought the solitude of the forests as much for aesthetic as for spiritual reasons.

It is even possible to claim the Buddha Himself for a poet. The Pali scriptures contain thousands of verses which are traditionally believed to have fallen from the lips of the master. One whole book, the *Udāna*, consists of a number of verses, each followed by a narrative in prose, of the circumstances which led to its composition, which the Buddha 'breathed out' (the literal meaning of the title-word) in moments of intense emotional pressure.

The bulk of the sacred canon, though prose in form, is frequently poetical in spirit. Enriched with vivid and appropriate metaphors, similes, parables, and other figures of speech, which delight the imagination as well as illumine the understanding, the discourses of the Buddha often glow with a subdued and serene loveliness which makes His words as beautiful as they are true. The undeniable fact that the Buddha and His enlightened disciples could appreciate and enjoy the beauty of nature and of art, and that they could even add to the sum of that beauty by their own aesthetic activities, is, we believe, sufficient proof of our contention that religion and art both are manifestations of the same movement of self-transcendence, and that the genuine devotee and the true artist travel along ultimately converging paths.

For the benefit of those who, though knowing that the

passages we have cited from the scriptures are authentic, may doubt whether the interpretation we have given of them is correct, we shall set the final seal of orthodoxy upon our views by quoting a modern writer of unquestionable reliability whose expositions of Buddhist doctrine are based on the strictest commentorial tradition. Referring to mental culture (*bhāvanā*), the second of the three stages into which, according to one scheme, the path to nirvana is divided, Dr C. L. A. de Silva says: 'The volitions arising in the processes of thought during the time of learning the Dharma Vinaya (the doctrine) or any arts, sciences, and so on too are included under the heading of mental culture or *bhāvanā*.'[16]

The inseparability of Buddhism and art arises out of the nature of our psychic life. Though will, intelligence, and emotion may be distinguished in thought from one another, and spoken of as if they were separate 'faculties', in reality they can no more be divided in this way than can the shifting green and gold and purple that shimmer on a pigeon's neck. Consequently, the spiritual development of man must either take place on all levels of his being, in all aspects of his personality, practical as well as theoretical, emotional no less than intellectual, or not at all. One 'part' of him cannot soar eagle-like in the empyrean, while another wallows pig-like in the mire; for ultimately there are no 'parts', and it is not piecemeal, but as a whole, that the life of man must either rise or fall in the scale of values. Spiritual practice—taking the expression in the widest sense, as whatever conduces to expansion of consciousness, to self-transcendence—must develop to the full all the 'faculties' with which human personality is endowed; and it must develop them not one-sidedly, but in a manner so harmonious that, at every stage of the spiritual ascent, they balance each other and approximate as nearly as possible to that condition of perfect equilibrium which will be theirs when consciousness has been expanded to its farthest limits, the ego utterly transcended.

Modern man, by which we mean modern western man and his imitators in eastern countries, suffers from a dissociation of intellect and emotion so chronic that it has almost paralysed his will for spiritual good. A kind of psychological elephantiasis has made him monstrous with an over-developed intellect and under-developed emotions. By this we do not mean that he is emotionally inactive; from from it! But that his emotional life, if so crudely spatial a metaphor may be pardoned, is on a much lower level than his intellectual life. His emotions are not non-existent, but undeveloped. Intellectually mature, he remains in feeling a child. The scientist, whose intellectual curiosity is not satisfied until he has numbered all the stars of the Milky Way, or measured as though with a rod the immensities of the heaven, seems to find full satisfaction for the affective side of his nature in the emotional muck-heaps of the popular film, in detective fiction, or in an occasional sexual embrace. One of the results of this rupture between the intellectual and the emotional life is that even the intellect is not developed with reference to a scale of values external to itself, but only with reference to the degree of its own internal complication. The need of modern man is, we conclude, for a development in his emotional nature which will render spiritually fruitful the intellectual development which has already taken place, and which will, by restoring the long lost equilibrium between his faculties, render possible for the whole personality that movement of ascent, of expansion of consciousness and self-transcendence, the secret of which seems to have been lost to Western civilization for so many centuries.

One of the normal instruments of emotional development in the past was religious devotion. But religion in the dogmatic Western Christian sense of the term has become so repugnant to modern man that the use of this instrument is often impossible. The discovery of some other means of refining his emotional life, therefore, becomes an imperative necessity. Such a method, we believe, may be found in the creation and enjoyment of works of art, provided that these activities are carried on with a vivid awareness of their spiritual function and significance. The desiderative nature of man clamours for satisfaction, and its demands cannot be ignored. If an outlet is not found for it on a higher level, then it will force one for itself on a lower. Sublimation of desire is, perhaps, the central problem of ethics, for sublimated desire is the dynamo that generates the energy whereby the machinery of the whole spiritual life is kept in motion. Art is important and valuable, in some cases even necessary, to the spiritual life, because it provides a channel for the emotional energies, leading them from lower to ever higher levels of expression. At each level the emotions galvanize the whole personality into activity; on the lower levels, into the innumerable activities whereby the ordinary man seeks to gratify his petty lusts and vanities; on the higher, as compassion, into the infinitely diverse expedients whereby Buddhas and Bodhisattvas seek to deliver mankind.

For the sublimation of the emotions, two things are necessary, a consciously imposed check on the lower, and a consciously opened outlet on the higher, levels of experience. The first is generally provided for the individual by the society in which he lives through a system of taboos. Of these taboos, the most important are those which, by checking the expression of the two primary emotions of love and hate, regulate the creative and destructive functions of emotion. Unfortunately, modern society often imposes the checks on one level without opening the outlets on the other. The individual, lacking any view of life which enables him to understand the possibility of attaining to a higher and wider kind of experience, is irritated by the constant imposition of what appear to him quite arbitrary checks to his natural impulses, and ultimately rebels against them. Psychological facts such as these help to explain a great deal of 'student indiscipline', juvenile delinquency, and other destructive manifestations of emotions that have been denied creative expression, and point to the necessity of giving a more prominent place in the educational curriculum to interests and activities by which the emotions are refined and sublimated. If the kind of education we receive should be determined, to some extent at least, by the kind of persons we are, and if emotion is agreed to be no less a component of human nature than reason, then no denial of the necessity of finding a place for art in the scheme of education can logically be made.

Inasmuch as the ideals governing the educational system of a given society are generated by the application, within the narrower field of educational theory and practice, of ideals that govern not only that society, but the whole civilization to which it belongs, it is to be expected that the absence of art today from our schools and colleges is but the reflection of a death of beauty in modern life. Since the Industrial Revolution, the cities in which the countries of the West have gradually concentrated their populations have been dominated by an ever increasing ugliness. Through political and commercial channels the products of this ugliness have flooded not only the Western but the Eastern world as well, and even now, high on the shores of traditional civilizations like those of India, Ceylon (Sri Lanka), and Burma, the retreating tide of imperialism has left a noisome deposit of ugliness which, putrefying in the tropic sun, continues to infect the lives of most oriental peoples. Modern man, whether of the East or of the West, is suffering from starvation of beauty, and until he again receives and assimilates that divine pabulum there is little hope of his being restored to spiritual health. Before World War II, the Moral Rearmament movement was launched in England. The inauguration on a global scale of a movement for Aesthetic Rearmament, the launching of a worldwide Battle for Beauty, is today no less necessary. Until an outlet for the emotions of man is found on those higher levels of experience, to which art and religion alike give access, they will continue on the lower their turbulent and destructive career. Like the two wings of a bird, reason and emotion are both indispensable to the spiritual flights of man.

Higher still and higher
From the earth thou springest
Like a cloud of fire;
The deep blue thou wingest,
And singing still dost soar, and
soaring ever singest.

The spiritual aspirant is like Shelley's Skylark: while his understanding soars, his emotions sing. It is in this singing and soaring, in the simultaneous expansion of the understanding and the emotions, that we find the meaning of Buddhism and the value of art, and, in fact, the secret of spiritual life.

The Religion of Art

The Religion of Art

Art and religion overlap. Just as there is in religion an element which is aesthetic, so there is also in art a constituent which is religious. In these days, when the decay of religious belief has led to the decline of that part of religion which is also a province of art, it might be possible, by developing the implications of that part of art which is also a province of religion, to promote a way of life dedicated to the realization of values in a manner attractive to those who are only repelled when it is presented to them from a formally religious point of view. It might even be possible to inaugurate for such people a Religion of Art.

By the Religion of Art we do not mean the use of art as one of the substitutes for religion in the Huxleian sense. Just as there are some things belonging to religion which have nothing to do with art, so also are there many things of much importance to art which have no place in religion. The coincidence between the areas of these two spheres of human activity is partial, not complete. Some religion is some art, and some art some religion. All religion is not all art. Mr Huxley makes it clear that while he uses the word religion in the fuller sense that includes an aesthetic constituent, the term art is used in the narrower sense that excludes any element of religion. Art-without-religion is set up as one of the substitutes of religion-with-art. Although admitting that 'to minds whose religious needs have been denied their normal fulfilment, art brings a certain spiritual satisfaction', the author of the penetrating essay on 'The substitutes for Religion' is not blind to the fact that 'Where beauty is worshipped for beauty's sake as a goddess, independent of and superior to morality and philosophy, the most horrible putrefaction is apt to set in', and he concludes his section on 'The Artistic Substitute' with the caustic observation 'The lives of the aesthetes are the far from edifying commentary on the religion of beauty'.[1]

The 'horrible putrefaction' which ensues when art is sundered from religion and metaphysics was the subject of a poem written almost a century earlier than Huxley's essay. In 'The Palace of Art' Tennyson has described with his usual abundance of vivid pictorial detail the fate of 'A Glorious Devil, large in heart and brain, That did love beauty only' and who had therefore planned to devote his life to the solitary enjoyment of whatever masterpieces of painting, music, and poetry had been produced by man. Historically speaking, the poem is prophetic of the Aesthetic Movement which was to spring up in the latter half of the nineteenth century, and which was to flower most gorgeously and most corruptly during the decade preceding the arrest and conviction of Oscar Wilde, when the dew was abruptly shaken from the black rose and the wasp-bodied butterflies rudely scattered from their green carnations. Psychologically, it is an eternally true study of the feelings of dissatisfaction and frustration into which a life of self-indulgence, even aesthetic self-indulgence, eventually disintegrates.

At the beginning of the poem, the 'glorious Devil' is described as building for his soul 'a lordly pleasure-house, Wherein at ease for ay to dwell', and is reported as inviting her to 'make merry and carouse'. She is to live alone in her high palace, indifferent to what is happening in the world outside, and caring nothing for the joys and sorrows of men. Indeed, to her fastidious taste the uncultured commonalty appears no better than 'darkening droves of swine', and with a little delicate shudder of disgust she watches them as they 'graze and wallow, breed and sleep'. But the day of retribution is at hand. The opium-eater's dream lasts but for three short years. In the fourth year, tormented by despair and doubt, she begins to loathe solitude and to hate herself. The pleasure-house becomes her prison; remorse scorches her like fire; and at the conclusion of the poem she abandons her palace for a cottage in the valley where she can 'mourn and pray'. She begs her master not to pull down her palace towers, which have been so lightly and beautifully built. It was not Art that was at fault, but the soul's misuse of Art. When she has purged her guilt, she says, perhaps it will be possible for her to return there and dwell, not alone, but this time in the company of other people.

Though 'The Palace of Art' is a poem, and not a treatise on ethics or an excursus into psychology, the moral which emerges from it's dream-like sequence of brilliant word-pictures is almost nakedly apparent, and has in fact been stated explicitly in the dedication which Tennyson prefixed to the poem. He that shuts out Love from his life shall in turn be shut out from Love,

And on her Threshold lie
Howling in outer darkness.

This is the sentence of what Buddhists would call *karma,* not blind fate or destiny, but that reaction of one's own action whereby the justice of the universe is asserted and the equilibrium of Nature restored. By love is meant not 'a meaty acquaintance' or a jealous emotional preference but that spirit of self-abnegation, that entire absence of selfish desires, which is the beginning and end of every virtue, the base and crown of all spirituality, and which according to Dante is so mighty that it 'moves the sun in heaven and all the stars'.

Though at a high stage of spiritual development it may be possible to speak, with Rilke, of 'love without the beloved', for most of us this emotion, like the rest, can be achieved only through our association with other men and women. The aesthete shuts out love from his life because he shuts out people, because his soul dwells 'alone unto herself' indulging in the refined selfishness of artistic pleasures. The sin he commits, the guilt which in the end he feels he must purge away, is the primal sin of attachment to one's separate selfhood. He finds to his horror that the much-vaunted doctrine of 'Art for Art's sake' is reversed in practice and becomes, though probably in a sense different from that intended by Lawrence, 'Art for my sake'. He discovers that he has failed to distinguish what have been called 'the pleasures of poetry', which first satisfy, then satiate, and finally disgust the soul, from 'the ardours of poetry', by which the soul is quickened, purified, and in the end liberated from the bondage of its own separateness. It is regarding works of art as an amusement, or employing them merely as a means of egoistic pleasure, that constitutes the distinguishing feature of Art as one of the Substitutes for Religion. The Religion of Art, on the contrary, views the creation and enjoyment of paintings, musical compositions, and poems as primarily a means of liberation from the egoistic life and looks upon Beauty as one of the three great initiators into the mysteries of the life of egolessness. But before attempting to gain a clear understanding of the nature of the Religion of Art we must first of all examine separately the meaning of Religion and the meaning of Art.

No one who has attempted to reduce into a semblance of order the swarm of indistinct ideas and confused emotions which cluster about 'religion' can have failed to be struck by the vagueness and ambiguity of this protean word. Like the Apostle to the Gentiles, it has endeavoured to be all things to all men; but instead of meaning something to everybody, it has now come perilously near to meaning nothing to anybody. In so thick an obscurity, indeed, has the word now become involved, that Mr Aldous Huxley, who introduces his collection of substitutes for religion with a description of what he calls 'the genuine article', very wisely refrains from attempting a formal definition of religion, remarking, 'Such definitions are mostly so vague and abstract as to be almost meaningless'. Instead of a definition he gives 'a catalogue of the principal states of mind and actions recognized as religious, together with a brief account of the most characteristic features of the religious doctrines which are the rationalizations of these states and acts'.[2]

'But recognized as religious by whom?' one may pertinently enquire. 'Most characteristic from what point of view, or in the eyes of which observer?' A description which highlights certain details of an object at the expense of certain others can be almost as misleading as a definition which submerges all alike in the double darkness of abstraction and generalization. Though not untrue, it does not tell the whole truth, and is therefore not wholly true. Moreover, description and definition cannot be divorced so absolutely as Mr Huxley's remarks appear to suggest. Definition is always of a specific thing which has been isolated for the purpose from the multiplicity of other things in the midst of which it exists. The isolation of a highly complex phenomenon like religion is impossible without some criterion of which elements are to be excluded and which are not. In other words, you cannot describe a thing unless you have first of all at least some knowledge of *what* is to be described. No description of religion can be attempted without formulating a provisional definition of the nature of religion. Such a provisional definition does in fact lurk somewhere at the back of Mr Huxley's mind, and betrays its presence as soon as he talks about 'rationalization'. Far from casting over the religions of the world a glance of Olympian impartiality, all that he offers us is a view of the subject which is asquint with selective prejudice. However, some of the characteristics he describes are undoubtedly characteristics of religion from the standpoint of the Religion of Art, and we shall therefore examine them one by one in the hope that this procedure will enable our own definition of the word to emerge with greater clearness. The description of 'the genuine article' which he has given in this essay certainly will be in any case more helpful to us than his researches in more recent years, which have extracted from the diversity of religious beliefs a Highest Common Factor as vague and abstract as the most impenitent intellectual, even, could wish for.

First in the Huxleian catalogue is 'A sense of awe in face of the mysteries and immensities of the world' which, he supposes, 'is the most fundamental religious state of mind'. The definition of religion implicit in his mind has already set in motion the machinery of selection, and by the time we have recovered from the jolt it is grinding away vigorously. 'This feeling is rationalized in the form of belief in supernatural beings, both kindly and malevolent, as is the world in which men live'. The wheels are now fairly whizzing round. 'In the higher religions the rationalization is very elaborate and constitutes an account, complete and coherent, of the whole universe'. The ambiguity of the word 'fundamental', which can be understood in a historical, psychological, or metaphysical sense, may be overlooked. What cannot be overlooked is the incompleteness of the facts whereon the generalization is based, and the consequent precariousness of an explanation reared on such a slender foundation. Like almost all generalizations about religion it ignores completely that vast area of belief and practice designated Buddhism. 'A sense of awe in face of the mysteries and immensities of the world' is not the 'fundamental' Buddhist state of mind in any sense of the word. Awe is a species of fear, and the fundamental Buddhist state of mind is

not one of fear, but of complete freedom from fear. All fear is basically hatred of death, just as every kind of hope is essentially desire for life. Desire and hatred, attraction and repulsion, are rooted in the ego-sense, in the false conception that the word 'self' denotes an unchanging entity separate from all other 'selves'. The fundamental Buddhist state of mind is a state of freedom from fear because it is also a state of freedom from the ego-sense. When the Buddha, before His Enlightenment, experienced a 'panic fear and dread' while dwelling alone in the terror-haunted jungle, so that the hair rose bristling on His scalp, He did not rationalize the feeling, as according to Mr Huxley He ought to have done, but remained where he was until He had subdued and conquered it. This spirit of 'heroic valour, firm and unmoved' He not only breathed Himself but inspired into the hearts of His disciples, and exercises for the control of fear have remained through the centuries an integral part of Buddhist spiritual practice. It is hardly reasonable to explain the beliefs of a religion as rationalizations of an emotion which it does its utmost to subjugate. Even a teaching that has suffered as much as Buddhism has from the misrepresentations of critics would not expect to be treated so unfairly. Though references to 'supernatural beings, both kindly and malevolent' do occur in the Tripitaka quite frequently, their occurrence cannot be regarded as a manifestation of awe in the face of natural phenomena on the part of the compilers of the sacred volumes. Without necessarily asserting the non- existence of 'supernatural' beings—a dogma which appears to be one of the Thirty-Nine Articles of modern 'scientific' belief—we would point out that such beings occupy an entirely subordinate position on the mythological fringe of Buddhism, so that even if their objective existence were definitely disproved the basic truths of the Dharma would remain unshaken. Indeed, it could be argued with considerable plausibility that the devas, yakshas, and other species of non-human beings who from time to time make their appearance in Buddhist apologue and anecdote are the rationalizations of the fears, not of the Buddha and His disciples, but of the peoples of pre-Buddhist India. The argument seems to be strengthened by the fact that even Mara, the chief of the malevolent beings, is never represented as a really dangerous or even formidable antagonist of the Buddha. He is a mischievous rather than an evil spirit, and totally lacks the dignity and grandeur of Milton's rebel angel. His wickedness vents itself by playing petty tricks and giving small annoyances; it does not explode in cosmic disaster or entail universal ruin. Like the emotions of which he and his myrmidons are supposed to be rationalizations, he is rendered harmless as soon as he is recognized, and has no refuge from ignominious punishment other than equally ignominious flight amid the laughter of the Arahants who are the witnesses of his discomfiture. Ridicule is a powerful solvent of fear, and the fact that they could laugh at the silly blundering wickedness of poor Mara shows that those early Buddhists were not afraid of him; perhaps it shows that they no longer really believed in his existence. The position occupied by the Prince of Darkness in the Pali scriptures is far from enviable. After all, it is not easy to tempt or frighten those who insist upon regarding you as a piece of obsolete psychology, or as an out-of-date literary convention.

Buddhism could, we suppose, without exaggerating its own importance, claim to rank among those 'higher religions' to which Mr Huxley's selective machinery rattles out a reference. But the inclusion serves only to make the uniqueness of the Dharma still more strikingly evident. Far from obediently toeing the line which Mr Huxley draws for the higher religions, and advancing a rationalization of the feeling of awe so 'very elaborate' that it constitutes 'an account, complete and coherent, of the whole universe', Buddhism withdraws into a position so aloof from that occupied by all other religions that some of them even consider it as no more belonging to their company. If interrogated on the subject it would agree (having in fact maintained the principle for five-and-twenty centuries) that complete and coherent accounts of the universe were if not all the direct outcome of fear, certainly at bottom the joint product of egoistic craving and ignorance. Indeed, being nothing if not practical, it would go much further than this and insist that all such accounts (*diṭṭhi,* or views, in its own terminology) must be abandoned if ever the mind is to attain to a condition of absolute freedom.

Buddhism is a method of resolving the disharmonies of life. In the oft-recurring formula of the sacred books, it teaches only 'suffering and the cessation of suffering'. It is not science, so that it has nothing to say concerning the origin of the material universe. It is not philosophy in the merely speculative or academic sense, so that it is silent on metaphysical differences which do not, in William James' expressive phrase, 'make a difference'. It is not religion in the Huxleian connotation of the term, because it not only fails to rationalize feelings of awe into a belief in good and evil spirits, but also refrains from elaborating them into a systematic explanation of the universe. Buddhism proclaims not merely freedom from fear, but also freedom from religion. For religion is based on fear. Needless to say, the belief in a personal Creator-God, which occupies a central position in all other higher religions, is regarded by Buddhism simply as a more ambitious, and therefore more harmful, result of the same process of rationalization which, at the other end of the scale, was responsible for the production of poor Mara. *Diabolus Deus inversus est.* Indeed Brahma cuts in the Pali Scriptures a figure no less ridiculous than that of his infernal counterpart, and for precisely the same reason. The fear of the Lord is, according to Buddhism, not the beginning of wisdom but the crown of folly. True wisdom cannot be attained until fear in all its forms has been conquered. What more effective means of dissipating this particular 'fear of the Lord' could there be than the delicate mockery of the Pali Scriptures?

The second item in Mr Huxley's catalogue of 'the principle states of mind and actions recognized as religious' is ritual. 'The religious feeling', he says, 'finds its active as opposed to its intellectual expression in the form of propitiatory ritual. Ritual, as soon as it is invented, occupies a position of prime importance in all religions. For the rite evokes by association those emotions of awe which are, for the individual who feels them, the God himself. And these emotions are accompanied by others no less exhilarating, and therefore no less divine. Chief among these is what may be called the social emotion, the feeling of excitement caused by being in a crowd'. Once again we are made aware of the enormous discrepancy between Buddhism and other religions. Gods and demons are, according to Mr Huxley, rationalizations of fear, and this feeling of fear is, as we have seen, absent from the representatively Buddhist mind. Yet, ignoring this fact, he rushes into a generalization to which, as the most elementary manual of Buddhism would have informed him, there is at least one very important exception, and sweepingly asserts that rituals for the propitiation of gods and demons occupy 'a place of prime importance in all religions', among which it must be supposed he intends to include Buddhism.

Let it be said at once that although such rituals are known in most Buddhist lands, and indeed are upon occasions resorted to by most Buddhists, they are merely survivals of primitive beliefs which have been affiliated to Buddhism, and in no sense form part of the original Dharma of the Buddha which, as we have already observed, on the contrary confines itself to resolving the disharmonies of life, to the attainment of a state of mind, usually designated Nirvana, whence fear and all other egocentric emotions have been prescinded.

Buddhist religious feeling finds its 'active as opposed to its intellectual expression' not in propitiatory ritual but in the practice of ethics (*śīla*), concentration (*samādhi*), and intuitive wisdom (*prajñā*); in following the Noble Eightfold Path which leads to Arahantship, and in cultivating the Ten Perfections of the Bodhisattva. It is a stranger to 'exhilarating' emotions of the Dionysian sort. What Mr Huxley calls 'the social emotion, the feeling of excitement caused by being in a crowd', far from being chief among Buddhist emotions, is deliberately excluded by it from their number. One of the signs by which the Dharma might be recognized, the Buddha told Mahapajapati, was that it conduced 'to solitude, not to company'. The bliss arising in the concentrated mind of the disciple is said, according to one interpretation of the word, to be 'born of solitude'. 'Wander alone, as the horn of the rhinoceros is single', sings the refrain of a poem in the *Sutta-Nipāta* which celebrates the delights of, and enumerates the spiritual advantages which accrue from, a life of solitariness. Not excitement but silence, the Aryan silence wherein not words merely, but also the perturbations of the mind, are stilled, is the emotion evoked by those assembled either in the presence of the Buddha or, after the disappearance of His earthly body, to do honour to His memory. When the physician Jivaka took Ajatasattu, the rajah of Magadha, on a nocturnal visit to the Master's Abode, so deep a silence surrounded the place that the King became suspicious and accused the physician of leading him into an ambush. The story is told with all the dignity and quiet beauty of the Pali Scriptures thus:

> Now when His Majesty Ajatasattu was close upon the Mango Grove, there came upon him fear and trembling, so that every hair upon his body stood on end, and he exclaimed to Jivaka: 'Surely, master Jivaka, you are deceiving me! Surely, master Jivaka, you are playing a trick

upon me! Are you not delivering me into the hands of mine enemies Jivaka?'

(Being reassured by Jivaka he went on) 'How is it, then, that there is not a sneeze, not a clearing of the throat, not a single sound to be heard in all this company of brethren, numbering (as you say) twelve hundred and fifty?'

'Fear not, Maharajah. Fear not, Maharajah. I am not deceiving your Majesty, nor playing you a trick, nor am I delivering your Majesty into the hands of your enemies. Go right on, Maharajah! Go right on, Maharajah! See! yonder in the pavilion the lamps are burning.'

Then the rajah went on, riding his elephant as far as the path allowed, then went on foot to the pavilion door. Then he said to Jivaka: 'Where, master Jivaka, is the Exalted One?'

'Yonder Maharajah, is the Exalted One! Yonder Maharajah, is the Exalted One, sitting up against the midpost pillar, facing east and surrounded by the brethren.'

Then the Rajah of Magadha, Ajatasattu, drew near to the Exalted One and stood aside. So standing he gazed upon that company sitting there in perfect silence, calm as a translucent pool. And he exclaimed: 'O that my boy Prince Udayi, the Lucky Lad, may be blessed with the peacefulness wherewith this company of brethren is now blessed!'[3]

The apprehensiveness of an ancient Indian despot, who went in constant fear of betrayal and assassination, is in this passage strikingly contrasted with the calm and untroubled bearing of the Buddha and His disciples who, far from abandoning themselves to 'the feeling of excitement caused by being in a crowd', were enjoying tranquillity of mind so great that the King could imagine for his darling son no blessing more desirable.

'Asceticism is common to all religions', says Mr Huxley of the third of his 'recognizedly' religious states of mind and actions. Had he ended with these words as well as begun with them, and permitted the reader to understand the word asceticism in whatever way he would, all had been well, and with one statement at least we should have had no cause for disagreement. Unfortunately, in the next sentence he makes it clear that by asceticism he means the belief that men could 'win the favour of the gods by abstaining from pleasure and comfort'. We have already shown that to the Buddha and His disciples the gods were not objects of fear, and from that for which no fear is felt obviously no attempt will be made to win favours. Abstention from pleasure and comfort for the mere sake of abstinence, or with the wrong view that self torture could lead to enlightenment, was one of the two kinds of extreme methods tried and rejected as useless by the Buddha, and was afterwards condemned by Him as 'painful, unworthy, and unprofitable' at the commencement of His first Sermon at Sarnath. The World-Honoured one taught instead a Middle Path which consists, on the level of ethics, in an equally scrupulous eschewal of self-indulgence and self-mortification. Mental purity can be won neither by pleasure nor by pain, but only by that special kind of wisdom—third of the three ascending stages into which the Noble Eightfold Path or Middle Way is divided—mention of which has already been made. Asceticism can be considered as an integral part of the Buddhist way of life, as a factor which contributes to the growth of wisdom, only if we use the word in its original Graeco-Roman sense of that 'training' or 'discipline' which, as J. Evola says, 'Aims at placing all the energies of the human being under the control of a central principle'.[4] This kind of asceticism is not confined to 'religion' but is one of the chief instruments whereby physical, intellectual, or artistic excellence of any kind is achieved. It is the blade which, pruning the exuberance of nature into the restraint of art (in the widest sense of the term), renders possible the unfolding of perfect blossoms of human culture. And Buddhism, it may be added, does not confuse the blade with the blossom. Asceticism is very definitely regarded only as a means to an end, and that this end has nothing to do with winning the favours of gods we now hardly need insist.

The next neatly cartoned product shot out by Mr Huxley's selective machinery is labelled 'future compensatory states' or, in plainer language, heavens and hells. Belief in the existence of these states or places he lays before us as 'one of the most typical religious doctrines', and accounts for its prevalence by saying, 'Human misery is so great and so widespread that one of the principal functions of religion has been that of consolation'. This explanation of course suffices only for the heavens, not for the hells. But be that as it may. The fact that human beings suffer has never been denied by Buddhism, which indeed on the contrary directs its attention primarily to 'pain and the cessation of pain'. However, though it teaches rebirth or 're-becoming' (*punabbhava*) after death, either in this world or another, the process of compensation goes on in strict accordance with the law of moral equity, whereby selfish volitions result in suffering, and unselfish ones in happiness. We are compensated not for what others have done to us but for that which we have done to others. Our sufferings on this earth, far from being in need of future compensation, are themselves generally the retribution of our misguided volitions in previous existences. Buddhist teaching on the subject of compensatory states can hardly be described as consolatory, in fact it can scarcely be described as essentially and specifically Buddhist. What may be termed the higher teaching of Buddhism points out that suffering is inseparable from sentient existence, and that true happiness is to be attained, not by seeking rebirth in any heaven-world, however glorious, but by eradicating that craving for continued individual existence which is the cause of rebirth, and by attaining, not after death but in this very life itself, the imperishable bliss of Nirvana.

'Absoluteness is a quality typical of religious beliefs', says Mr Huxley of the fifth item in his catalogue. 'Religious doctrines are held with a passionate tenacity. If what is believed is absolutely true, then it is of vital importance that the believer should cling to his belief and refuse to admit the contrary beliefs of others. Conversely, absoluteness of belief, resulting from whatever cause, tends to create a certainty of the absolute reality of the thing believed in. The quality of the faith is transferred to its object, which thereby becomes absolute and consequently worthy of worship'. Nowhere else, perhaps, does Buddhism so clearly tower with supreme transcension above all other 'religions' than when it teaches, not the absoluteness, but the relativity, of all religious beliefs and practices whatever, its own included. Of the supreme experience of Nirvana no attribute can be predicted, no quality affirmed. All that can be said is that certain beliefs and practices conduce to its achievement, while others do not. The former are collectively termed 'Dharma', which is the correct word for what is popularly called 'Buddhism'; the latter Adharma, or that which is contrary to Dharma. Far from encouraging His disciples to hold His doctrines 'with a passionate tenacity' the Buddha time and time again reminded them that, in the words of the famous 'Parable of the Raft', the Dharma was 'something to leave behind, not to take with you'.[5] One who thought that ethics, concentration, and wisdom were ends in themselves, and not simply a means for the attainment of Nirvana, and who endowed them with absolute value, was in His opinion no less foolish than a man who, after crossing a great river, should bear away on his shoulders the raft whereon he had paddled over, instead of hauling it up onto the shore, or sinking it in the water and going about his business. Since for the Buddhist none of his own beliefs is 'absolutely true', it is not of vital importance that he 'should cling to his belief and refuse to admit the contrary beliefs of others'. Typical as this attitude is of the followers of other 'religions', it is quite unfamiliar to those who truly follow the Buddha.

The Buddhist attitude is that of the sharp sighted man in another parable, the 'Parable of the Elephant', who saw with a smile of amusement six blind men disputing about the nature of that lordly pachyderm, one seizing its trunk and declaring it to be like a serpent, another grasping its ear and maintaining that it resembled a winnowing-basket, and so on one after the other until they all fell into a rage and began fighting among themselves.[6] 'Views' are, in Huxleian language, rationalizations of egocentric emotions, and Enlightenment cannot be attained until they are abandoned. Even 'Right Views', the intellectual formulation of the conditions precedent to the attainment of Nirvana, are not to be understood as metaphysically true or clung to as though they possessed absolute validity, but simply to be used with discrimination for the attainment of those ends to which they are in the nature of things best adapted. Absoluteness of belief being absent from Buddhism, there is no question of it tending to create 'a certainty in the absolute reality of the thing believed in'. The kind of 'faith' and 'worship' ensuing from this certainty are therefore meaningless words to it.

Almost equally meaningless, from the Buddhist point of view, is the word 'priest', despite the fact that Mr Huxley introduces the last item of his catalogue with the generalization 'All religions have priests, who fulfil a double function.' 'They are', proceeds his description, 'in the first place, to use M. Paul Valéry's expressive phrase, *les preposes aux choses vagues*—mediators between man and the surrounding mystery, which they understand and can propitiate more effectually than ordinary folk. Their second function is earthly; they are confessors, advisers, casuists, spiritual doctors; at certain periods they have also been rulers'. Though 'priest' is hardly a correct rendering of the Aryan word *bhikshu,* which originally meant a mendicant friar, the life of the bhikshu has two aspects which are in a sense analogous to the double function which, according to Mr Huxley, priests fulfil. He 'mediates between man and the surrounding mystery' not by propitiating malevolent beings on man's behalf, but by revealing through his own actions the greatest of all mysteries, the mystery of holiness. The bhikshu mediates between the ideal and the real, and enables mankind to see the highest spiritual truths in terms of ordinary human life. He does more than this. By his practical instructions he enables people to know the mystery of holiness for themselves; he helps them make it a part of their own experience. In this twofold way, combining example and precept, he makes the mystery to them a mystery no longer, and irradiates the darkness of the unknown with the light of realization.

It has been truly said that a complete account of Buddhism could be given by simply denying one after another the statements made about it by non-Buddhist writers. Similarly, we have allowed our own descriptions of 'the principal states of mind and actions recognized as religious' to emerge into view by laying bare the shortcomings of Mr Huxley's account of them. These shortcomings are all due to the fact that in spite of his disparagement of formal definitions of religion he had lurking at the back of his mind a definition which was not broad enough to include Buddhism. The exclusion is significant, though with the exploration of that significance we are not now concerned. We are concerned instead with the discovery of a definition of religion which will be of service to us in our task of making clear the nature of the Religion of Art. Such a definition will necessarily deal not with adventitious frills and trimmings but with the barest essentials of the thing, and even those essentials it must present, not in incipient or half-developed shapes, but only in the perfection of their fully articulated forms. If it should be objected that our attempt to elicit a definition of religion from a consideration of Mr Huxley's catalogue was in fact nothing but an exhibition of the differences, both partial and complete, by which Buddhism is separated from all other faiths, we shall reply that such a proceeding was unavoidable, because Buddhism is not merely a religion among religions, but Religion in its classical and archetypal form, disentangled from all irrelevant additions, so that a complete unfolding of the characteristics of religion inevitably results in a description of what, historically speaking, is the Dharma of the Buddha. The truth of this statement may be made more evident by abstracting our observations from their Huxleian context and presenting them as an independent description of recognizably religious states and actions, after which we shall allow the rotundities of description to crystallize into the straighter lines and acuter angles of one of those abstract definitions which Mr Huxley affected so much to despise. Our own catalogue, then, is briefly as follows.

The fundamental religious state of mind is a sense of absolute fearlessness. This feeling is the result of freedom from selfish attachments and desires, which is itself the consequence of having abandoned the misconception that one is essentially a separate, unchanging individual being. Interpretations of existence which have been elaborated from rationalizations of egocentric emotions such as hope and fear dissolve like mist, and the emancipated mind shines forth in its intrinsic purity unclouded by even the shadow of a concept.

The religious feeling finds its active as opposed to its theoretical expression in the practice of ethics, the development of the mind through concentration, and the intuitive realization of higher wisdom, all of which are necessary steps on the path leading to liberation from the ego-idea and, consequently, to those emotions of fearlessness which are, for the individual who feels them, a proof of the authenticity of his realization. These emotions are accompanied by others no less tranquillizing, and therefore no less genuinely spiritual. Chief among these is what may be called the solitary emotion, the feeling of bliss and peace caused by being alone.

Asceticism is not an end in itself, but only a means of concentrating the total energies of the personality along a single line of development. Self-torture is not only of no use in the spiritual life, but is even positively harmful.

Human suffering is the result of selfish desires, of craving, and can cease only when those desires cease. Rebirth in a heaven after death, as the result of living virtuously, is possible, but since such a state is not everlasting, being subject to the universal law of impermanence, it also is eventually a source of suffering. Permanent happiness, the happiness of Nirvana, can be obtained in this life itself by the destruction of craving.

Relativity is a quality typical of religious beliefs. Religious doctrines should be followed but they should never be made a basis of attachment. If what is believed is only relatively true, then it is of vital importance that the believer should not cling to his belief and refuse to admit the contrary beliefs of others. Conversely, tentativeness of belief, resulting from whatever cause, tends to create a conviction of the merely relative and instrumental value of religious doctrines and practices. Faith is belief in the efficacy of the means employed after we have put them to the test in our own life and experience. It is 'confidence based on knowledge'.

Buddhism is the only religion which has bhikshus, who fulfil a double function. They are in the first place living embodiments of the Buddhist ideal, and in the second the teachers of that ideal to the world in general, and the Buddhist community in particular, as well as the conservators of the entire great heritage of Buddhist culture, the whole body of which collectively, and each part individually, is intended as a means of orienting human life in the direction of its highest goal.

Having now given our own description of the archetypally religious states of mind and actions, it will not be difficult for us to telescope them into a definition of religion. The central principle stands out among the multiplicity of its applications with unmistakable pre-eminence. Religion is essentially the experience of egolessness; the truly religious life is the life of egolessness; and genuinely religious beliefs and practices are those by which the realization of egolessness can be achieved. Like most definitions, this one that we have given of religion is abstract and contentless in the extreme, and although nobody, perhaps, would be inclined to deny its correctness, not one of them, probably, would find it of much practical use. Definition is the result of comparison, abstraction, and generalization, all of which are intellectual operations. Warm, living, concrete things are fed into one end of the intellectual machine and emerge at the other cold, dead concepts with every drop of emotion squeezed out of them. These concepts reason may manipulate in a ghastly puppet-dance of argument, spinning round her 'bloodless ballet of unearthly categories' in a complicated choreography of syllogisms; but though the performance may convince the head, it is powerless to move the heart. The heart can be moved only by emotions, and only the heart can move man. Intellectual recognition of the fact that religion consists in a life of egolessness is not sufficient to inspire anyone actually to live such a life, because his emotional energies have not been involved. To know what is good is not the same as to do what is good because, as Aristotle remarked in his unanswerable criticism of the ethical theory of Socrates, it fails to take into consideration 'the irrational parts of the soul'. Every religion therefore attempts, not only to justify its teachings to the intellect, but also to recommend them to the feelings. Through myth, ritual, literature, painting, sculpture, and music each tries to canalize emotion into the arid fields of the doctrines in which they wish us to believe and the practices they desire us to follow. In this way arises what is generally known as religious art. But, as might be expected, an ambiguity lurks in the word 'religious', and in order not to be confused by it we shall have to bear in mind the description of truly religious mental states and practices we have already given, and the definition of religion which we elicited from that description. Religious art is that kind of poetry, music, painting, or any other species of art, which conduces to the experience of egolessness. Much conventionally religious art, particularly Christian art, is not religious art in the sense that we have defined the term because it not only fails to induce the experience of egolessness, but even positively strengthens the ego-sense. The kind of pseudo-religious art that we have in mind is represented by sensually attractive Madonnas such as the Italian Renaissance painters so abundantly produced, and by literary works such as the *Rāmacharitamānasa* of Tulsidas, which despite its poetical beauties is only the hot air of devotional frenzy inflating the bladder of brahminical egoism. The direct contrary of such pseudo-religious art, which is religious in subject but non-religious in sentiment, is what may be termed naturally or essentially religious art, which is religious in sentiment, though non-religious in subject. Examples of this kind of art might be multiplied indefinitely: Chinese landscape painting, the best of Shelley's poetry, and much of the music of Beethoven, are sufficient to represent it. Two more permutations of the terms 'religious art' and 'non-religious art' it is possible to obtain. The first of these is religious both conventionally and naturally, in subject as well as sentiment, while the second is religious in neither, a work of art of this type being merely a profane subject profanely treated. The Buddha-image is perhaps the finest example of the one, and almost all contemporary popular art among the worst examples of the other.

Further refinements of classification it would be possible to introduce, but since they are irrelevant to our present purpose we abstain from making them. Of the four categories of Art already mentioned our concern is with the second only, for it is this which supplies the raw material, as it were, of the Religion of Art. We are not concerned with art-works of the first category because their ostensible religiosity often prevents them from appealing to modern sensibility, while their lack of truly religious sentiment—their failure to impart the experience of egolessness—renders them valueless from the point of view adopted in our present enquiry. With the fourth kind of art we have no concern not only because it is not in any sense religious, but because it is perhaps only superficially art. The domain of the Religion of Art, as demarcated at the beginning of our enquiry, is that province of art which is also a province of religion, and that part of true religion which is also a part of art. But before attempting to deal with the Religion of Art it will be necessary for us to deal separately with the nature of art, just as we had already to deal separately with the nature of religion.

Art is essentially creative. Like the general creativity of human life, civilization, and culture, of which it is the highest and most intensified development, it creates, not out of nothing, but by impressing its own ideal forms upon the chaos of sensuous experience. The *materia prima*, the stuff and raw material that an artist subdues and adapts to his creative purpose, is compounded of outlines, colours, masses, words, and sounds with which all men are familiar, and which are indeed themselves products of the rudimentary artistic activity if not of humanity at least of an important section of the human race. These sensuously given elements the painter, sculptor, poet, and musician organize into formal relations which, by some mysterious resonance of the human spirit, are capable of imparting a pleasure more intense and rare than that given by sensuous experiences which have not been so organized. But however intense the pleasure given by works of art it would be a mistake to suppose that art gives nothing but pleasure. Poetry, for example, which is the most fully developed form of art, even as Buddhism is the archetypal form of religion, is not only pleasurable but meaningful: besides expressing the poet's emotions it communicates his sense of values. It is the organ not merely of his feelings, much less still only of his thoughts, but of the whole unified sensibility with which he explores undiscovered regions of experience. Though the terms 'sensibility' and 'experience' have been allowed to stand for the subjective and objective aspects of artistic realization it should not be thought that a rigid line of demarcation can be drawn between them. Experiences are not possessions like pieces of furniture, but states and modifications of our own being, or, in more Buddhistic language, of our own *becoming.* The poet experiences things directly, by assimilating them into his spiritual being in much the same way as he assimilates material food into his physical body. For this reason some philosophers of art have thought that art was adequately defined as intuition, in which the subject and object of experience coalesce as it were into one. What the poet, or any other artist, tries through his special medium to express is not so much an unfamiliar kind of experience as a new mode of being. As Rilke says at the end of his sonnet 'Archaic Torso of Apollo'

Here is no place That does not see you.
You must change your life.[7]

The 'you' to whom the poet addresses his exhortation is what Indian Aesthetics has termed the *rasika* (a much better word than either the 'aesthete' or 'critic' of European artistic tradition), the 'taster' or 'enjoyer' of the *rasa* or aesthetic relish which saturates a work of art. For art is not only expression but communication as well. According to Herbert Read it communicates a sense of values.[8] Values are things that are desirable not as means to the attainment of other things, but for their own sakes. Modes of being or states of consciousness (in Buddhist philosophy being and consciousness are equated) which are expressed in, and communicated by, works of art, are not values from the point of view of the artist—for he has already attained them—but only to his audience, who are first of all startled into an enhanced awareness of life by the impact of a sensibility infinitely more refined and powerful than their own, and then confronted with the terrible necessity of renouncing their old self and transforming it into a new personality by the assimilation of a wholly unfamiliar experience. Often they shrink from what their natural egoism regards as the stress and pain of such transformation. They feel only the terror of death, and not the joy of birth into a richer and larger life. J. B. Leishman compares the lines which we have just quoted from Rilke with the description in the poet's *Malte Laurids Brigge* of a certain actress, probably Eleonora Duse, who 'Tried to distract the gaze of the audience from herself to the immense reality that filled her. *But they were already breaking into applause in their terror of the extreme: as though at the last moment to deflect from themselves something that would compel them to change their lives'.*[9]

At this stage of our enquiry, which has now brought us to the point at which the realm of art begins to overlap the realm of religion, we may fittingly condense our findings into a formal definition of the nature of art before attempting to gain admittance to the fascinating domain of the Religion of Art or to continue our journey through its unexplored interior. *Art is the organization of sensuous impressions into pleasurable formal relations that express the artist's sensibility and communicate to his audience a sense of values that can transform their lives.* The completeness of this definition becomes clearly apparent when we compare it with fragmentary definitions according to which art is 'an attempt to create pleasing forms' (Herbert Read), 'significant form' (Clive Bell), or, most simply of all, 'intuition' (Croce). It moreover illuminates the significance of definitions of beauty as modern as Herbert Read's 'Beauty is the unity of formal relations among sense perceptions', or as ancient as the scholastic 'Beauty is the splendour of form reflected on the proportioned parts of matter'.

Having now formed a clear, even if rather abstract, idea of the nature of religion and the nature of art as independent lines of human activity, we must now trace out the parallels between them, as well as determine, if possible, their exact points of intersection. First of all we shall have to examine the relation between egolessness and art; but the examination will be fruitful only if we load every rift of our conception with the ore of concrete meaning.

In spite of its negative form, the word egolessness, or in unmixed Anglo-Saxon unselfishness, is far from devoid of positive content, as we shall presently see, though our effort to reveal that content may well begin with an explanation of the principle which it negates. This principle, strange to say, is in truth itself a negation, a suppression of reality; that is to say, it is a delusion. The ego does not really exist; it is not a thing but a thought; not a metaphysical entity but an epistemological error. It is simply the idea of separate individuality. Since ideas are themselves things (not in the sense of being material objects, but in the sense that they are capable of producing tangible effects) the idea of separate individuality does not remain ineffectually floating about in the ether of consciousness but descends upon the earth in a storm of consequences. Being a wrong idea it proliferates effects which are wrong. The first of these effects is the attraction and aggregation of material particles into a human body endowed with sense-organs through which the ennucleating 'ego' will be able to gratify that craving for individual existence, that longing for experience as a separate 'self', which it has carried over unsatisfied from previous births and which is the cause of its present 'reincarnation'. In this new body it experiences sensations that enhance its feeling of separateness, and sensations which diminish it and even threaten the existence of its physical basis. The former it describes as pleasurable, the latter as painful. These simple sensations of pleasure and pain are connected with the idea of external cause, and in this way the automatic responses of attraction and repulsion are transformed into conscious desire and aversion, together with all the elaborate variations and permutations of these two great feelings which constitute the self-centred emotional life of ordinary people.

Since men live not in solitude but in society their efforts to maintain and augment their own separate selfhood inevitably bring them into conflict with all the millions of other men who are engaged in the same attempt. Interests differ, and therefore individualities necessarily clash. Different social groups come into conflict with one another. 'Religions' disagree, and holy wars are preached. National existences are threatened, and armies march to the battle-field. Bodies of men, women, and children are hideously mutilated or blown to pieces. Blood flows like a river. The details of such scenes of human conflict are nowadays too familiar to require further particularization. As Spinoza long ago understood, individuals, nations, and all other things, endeavour to persist in their own mode of being, or, as we should ourselves phrase it, to prolong their own stream of becoming, to go on repeating, over and over again, the same old pattern of experience. The colours may vary from time to time, the threads be changed from coarse to fine, but all are woven into the same unchanging pattern. If (to use a more dynamic metaphor) some new experience rushes comet-like from the unknown immensity of the surrounding universe, the ego steadies itself grimly on its axis, and, putting forth all its powers of attraction, endeavours to draw the intruder from his path and swing him round like a planet at the circumference of its own little solar system.

Selfishness is simply unwillingness to face new experiences. A radically new experience which we cannot weave into the pattern of our life demands the changing of the pattern and the working out of a fresh design in which it can form a part. The ego resists the onrush of new experiences because of the changes they involve; for a change in experience means a modification of existence; and though, in relation to the new life, such a modification is a birth, in relation to the old life, to the ego, it is in fact a death. Unselfishness, on the other hand, is an openness to new experiences, a willingness to die for the sake of being born anew. If egoism is a centripetal tendency, a movement of contraction upon its own centre, egolessness, on the contrary, is a centrifugal tendency, a movement of expansion not only towards its own circumference (for this has no meaning except in relation to a centre) but towards something absolutely outside the orbit of its own being. If a new experience appears comet-like in the sky, it eagerly abandons its own planetary system and spins towards it singing, with Shelley's Moon,

I must hurry, whirl and follow,
Through the heavens wide and hollow.[10]

This is the spirit of the true artist. Possessing from his birth an extraordinary sensitiveness to what Wordsworth called 'unknown modes of being'—a capacity to experience what Mr Aldous Huxley, writing of D. H. Lawrence, describes as 'the dark presence of the otherness that lies beyond the boundaries of man's conscious mind'—he is passionately eager to widen and deepen the range of his experience to the farthest possible limit.

Now experience is of two kinds: that which relates to the external world of flowers, trees, people, mountains, and stars; and that which relates to the internal world of emotions, thoughts, imaginations, and intuitions. Our use of the words 'widen' and 'deepen' refers to the possibility of developing experience in these two directions. The artist widens his experience by continually increasing the number of his points of contact with the material universe in which he lives; for, like Anteus in the myth, contact with the earth strengthens him. He deepens his experience (or heightens it, for both words connote refinement and intensification) first of all by becoming aware of it and then by subjecting it to a process of prolonged incubatory reflection in which essentials are separated from accidents and the significance of the experience gradually disclosed.

Contact with the earth is of course possible only through the body, by means of the five senses, particularly the eye, and to the poet's awareness through this highly sensitive organ of what we have elsewhere described as 'the unique individuality of things' we have already given the name Observation.[11] When an object is observed intently for some time sympathy for it will begin to be felt, for in the act of pure observation self-awareness is suspended and, at least for an instant, subject coalesces with object and feels the pulse of its existence beating indistinguishably from its own. Contact with 'unknown modes of being', on the other hand, is possible not through any external sense but only through an internal organ of experience—by means of refined and subtilized emotion. As we have explained in our *Advice to a Young Poet*, emotion, which is a force, can be subtilized by what we have there called the asceticism of art, wherein conscious inhibition of the normal outlets of emotional energy succeeds in making it seek expression on higher and more refined levels of existence.[12]

Though we have spoken of the two kinds of experience, one having the external, the other the internal, world for object, it should not be supposed that they exist side by side without any deeper or more intimate relation than that of mere external juxtaposition. They are not so much two worlds as two hemispheres of experience within the one world of the artist's personality. Between these two hemispheres a continual traffic goes on. Facts are forever crossing over into our personal life as feelings, and experiences which are both thoughts and feelings, as well as something more significant than either, go forth into the external world not as fugitive words and deeds but as immortal works of art. The poet (to change the metaphor) is rooted in the objective world as a plant is rooted in the soil. The nutriment which he derives therefrom is transformed into the invisible sap of aesthetic experience and creative potency, re-emerging thence into visibility not as earth and water but as the marvel of a leaf or the miracle of a flower. For the true poet seeks not only to enrich his experience through observation of, and sympathy with, life in all its multitudinous forms, but also to refine it, to raise it to the highest possible pitch of intensity, by solitary reflection on its meaning. Poetry which has not been enriched by the continual influx of sensuous impressions lacks vitality, while that which has not been refined by prolonged meditation is drossy and impure, and incapable of imparting to the *rasika* that sudden shock of delight which transports him into a hitherto unknown region of experience. The rhythm of the poet's life is dominated by the systole and diastole of receptiveness and creativity, absorption and transmutation, enrichment and refinement. Sometimes his heart expands until it embraces the universe; sometimes it contracts into a point. Both movements are necessary, and the soul of the poet can no more exist with one only than his physical body can live with a heart that only pumps blood in or only pumps it out.

The first kind of poetic experience, the necessity for that subtle alchemy whereby objective fact is transmuted not merely into subjective feeling but into the very stuff of the poet's personal life, has found poignant utterance in Rilke's well known description of poetry in *The Notebook of Malte Laurids Brigge*:

> But alas! [he exclaims] one does not get very far with verses if one writes them too early. One should wait and collect sense and sweetness during a whole lifetime and if possible a long one, and then, right at the end, one might perhaps be able to write ten lines that were good. For verses are not, as people suppose, feelings (one has them soon enough)—they are experiences. For the sake of a verse one must see many cities, men, and things, one must know animals, one must feel how birds fly, and understand the gestures with which little flowers open in the morning. One must be able to look back upon roads in unknown regions, on unexpected meetings and on partings that one long foresaw, on days of childhood that are still unexplained, on parents whom one had to hurt, if they brought one a pleasure and one did not comprehend it (it was a pleasure for someone else)—on childish illnesses, that begin so strangely with so many deep and difficult changes, on days in still, subdued rooms and on mornings by the sea, on all that the sea can mean, on seas, on nights of travel that rushed away on high and flew with all the stars—and even if one is able to think of all that, it is not yet sufficient. One must have memories of many nights of love, of which not one was like another, of cries of women in labour and of light, white sleeping women in childbed, who are closing. But one must also have been beside the dying, must have sat beside the dead in the room with the

open window and the intermittent sounds. And still, even to have memories is not sufficient. If there are many of them one must be able to forget them, and one must have the great patience to wait till they return. For the memories themselves are not yet what is required. Not till they become blood within us, look and gesture, nameless and no longer distinguishable from ourselves, not till then is it possible, in some very rare hour, for the first word of a verse to arise in their midst and to proceed from them.[13]

The second kind of experience, the indispensable complementary process in which the enriched poetic personality is elevated to hitherto unscaled heights of being by the deliberate refinement of its emotional energies, has been admirably described by J. B. Leishman in his Commentary on *Later Poems*.

Here we have the very kernal of what might be called Rilke's philosophy of love. He felt that the immense reserve of emotional energy developed or released by that experience ought not to be squandered on a transient and comparatively trivial satisfaction, but suppressed, repressed, damned up like a stream, until it reached an almost unbearable intensity, and then used as the propulsive force for some journey to the infinite, to undiscovered regions of thought and feeling. It might, perhaps, be objected that here art was encroaching upon life; that, while the exhortation to sublimate his emotional experiences, to divert and convert them into means of imaginative discovery and creation, may be valid for the artist, it is only partially valid for humanity in general. I feel there is something in this objection, but, at the same time, I also feel that (like many other objections to Rilke) it tends to flatter too much our satisfaction with ourselves as we are.[14]

Inasmuch as love is the basic emotion, even as desire is the fundamental feeling (love being, according to Spinoza, pleasure accompanied by the idea of an external cause), Rilke's philosophy of love is no less a philosophy of all the emotions, and his technique of sublimation can therefore be applied not to one emotion alone but to the whole affective life. This process of sublimation is for the artist not only valid, but an indispensable part of his artistic experience. If it is only partially valid for humanity in general the reason is that ordinary men and women are only partially artists. Their sensibilities are coarse, their imagination weak, and their creative power constantly frittered away on 'transient and comparatively trivial satisfaction'. Whatever their nominal religion may be, such people more often regard their physical body as the centre of the universe, and the gratification of the senses, together with the occasional titillation of the lower mind, as the highest aim of existence. As yet no spark of divine discontent has fallen from the stars to set their hearts ablaze. The winds of spirit search for them in vain from end to end of the sky. They sit snug all the while in the cosy cottage of individual selfhood, huddling over the smoky flame of desire, and are quite content to be shuttered in from the airs of truth that blow so clean and cold outside. Any interruption of the 'noiseless tenor of their way', to say nothing of any quickening of their dormant spiritual life, or any drastic modification of their own being, is farther from their thoughts than flying to the moon. They do not want to change their lives; they are, as Leishman phrases it, satisfied with themselves as they are. Most human beings are content to be human beings, just as a pig is content to be a pig, and long indeed is the coming of that 'spiritual dawn' when

By vengeful working of mysterious codes
An angel wakens in the drowsy beast.[15]

That dawn can come either from Religion or from Art (in the

sense that we have defined them), and one might as well blame light for encroaching on darkness as object to art that it encroaches upon life. It is the function of art to encroach upon life. For a great work of art embodies an unfamiliar experience, and this experience confronts us, as the archaic torso of Apollo confronted Rilke, with a challenge and a demand, with the flat imperative: 'You must change your life'. If in our terror we refuse to accept that challenge, to meet that demand, then the world of art is in reality closed to us. Then we either have not intercourse with it at all, or else attempt to enjoy works of art without permitting them to transform our lives. In the first case we become philistines, in the second aesthetes of the type satirized in 'The Palace of Art'. Tennyson's 'glorious Devil large in heart and brain That did love Beauty only' was simply a man who thought of art as a comparatively refined means of sensuous pleasure, as a elegant cup-bearer at the feast of life, rather than as a bare skeleton grimly announcing the necessity of terrible transformations. (Death and art are terrible for the same reason: both represent change.)

Religion, we have already seen, is essentially a life of egolessness; and egolessness, we have found, is fundamentally a willingness to accept new experiences. The Religion of Art may therefore be defined as conscious surrender to the Beautiful, especially as manifested in poetry, music, and the visual arts, as a means of breaking up established egocentric patterns of behaviour and protracting one's experience along the line of egolessness into the starry depths of Reality. It will be noted that we speak not merely of experiences but of new experiences, for only a new experience is capable of making a breach in that thick wall of selfhood with which most of us are surrounded. By 'new' we do not mean, however, the relative newness of, for instance, a young man's first experience of love, which is new only to him, but of what is, within the limits of average human experience, the absolute newness of a symphony of Beethoven or a sonnet by Keats.

According to some ancient Indian poets the essential quality of Beauty is that it remains from moment to moment ever new *(tadeva rūpam ramaṇīyaṭāyāh ksaṇe ksaṇe yanavaṭāṁ vidhaṭṭe).*[16] Since every new experience compels a fresh modification of character it might be possible to describe Beauty not only as that which is always new, but also as that which, far from allowing us the luxury of remaining satisfied with ourselves as we are, demands from moment to moment a fresh transformation of our lives. Absolute Beauty (to plunge for a minute into the stormy sea of metaphysics) would then be that Beauty whose demands upon us are inexhaustible, which never allows us to rest in any perfection, and which even beyond what seems to us the highest transformation calls for another higher still.

This conception of the aesthetic life as being fulfilled in a perpetual progress, rather than in a definite arrival at a fixed point of achievement, is paralleled by an Early Buddhist teaching the significance of which was first emphasized by Dr Beni Madhab Barua in his lecture on *Buddhism as Personal Religion.* According to this teaching (which though attributed to the nun Dhammadinna, was approved by the Buddha Himself),

> Buddha's Causal Genesis admits of two different trends of things in the whole of reality. In one of them the reaction (*paṭibhāga*) takes place in a cyclical order between two opposites (*paccanīkas*), such as pleasure and pain (*sukha-dukkha*), virtue and vice (*punnapāpa*), good and evil (*kusala-akusala*). This is aptly termed by Buddhaghosa as *visabhāga-paṭibhāgas.* In the other, the reaction takes place in a progressive order between two counterparts or complements, or between things of the same genus the succeeding factor augmenting the effect of the preceding one. This is what Buddhaghosa terms *sadisa-paṭibhāga.* By the term 'world', as distinguished from Nirvana, we are to

> understand the first trend in the Causal Genesis where we revolve within the cycle of reaction between the opposites. Nirvana represents the other trend in the Causal Genesis in which the course of reaction lies from strength to strength, good to further good, from that to still greater good, from pleasure to joy, from joy to gladness, from gladness to happiness, from happiness to bliss, from bliss to beatitude, from intuitional knowledge (*vijjā*) to the feeling of emancipation (*vimutti*), from that to self-mastery (*vasībhāva*) or self-consciousness as to the acquisition of the free state, and from that to the fullest enjoyment of the bliss of Nirvana. In reply to the question as to what follows by way of reaction from Nirvana Dhammadinna wisely said that Nirvana was generally regarded as the final step of the process in order to avoid an infinite regress—for the sake of *pariyantagahaṇam* in her own language. But she has not failed to indicate that even if there lie any further reaction, that also takes place in the line and that whatever follows therefrom will also appertain to Nirvana and, therefore, will partake of its nature.[17]

Less than five hundred years after Dhammadinna these ideas received their full development in the *Prajñāpāramitā Sūtras,* wherein the principle of infinite regress is accepted, and wherein the Bodhisattva is time and again exhorted not to rest in any dharma, not to regard any attainment as ultimate, including the attainment of Nirvana, and wherein he is in fact even required to abandon the idea of attainment altogether. The greatest mistake an aspirant to the life of egolessness could make would be to think of egolessness as though it was a kind of attainment. For it is not so much a state or an experience as an attitude to all states and experiences whatsoever. This attitude reveals itself as a readiness to renounce old experiences and to face and embrace new ones. Egolessness is thus not any state of existence, howsoever exalted, but essentially a condition of will. Neither the saint nor the artist—the artist in goodness nor the saint of the beautiful—should allow himself to become attached to his experiences, attainments, or realizations. For to rest in any particular experience of the good, or of the beautiful, would mean nothing less than the collapse of his spiritual or aesthetic career.

Art adores that Absolute Beauty which, since it is ever new, demands of its votaries the perpetual transformation of their lives, offering as reward for the terror of incessant death the joy of repeated birth into a life infinitely enriched and refined 'beyond all that is comprehensible and embraceable here.'[18] It does not allow them to settle down in any perfection, for, as Lama Govinda has pointed out, perfection itself is not 'an absolute value or a fixed condition', and 'neither exists as an end at the top of a scale, nor as an absolute or fixed measurement, but as an infinitesimal moment of harmony in movement'.[19] The true artist understands this relativity of perfection no less thoroughly than the true saint does. He beholds beauty rising and shining beyond beauty as the mountaineer sees range upon range of hills rising up one behind another, each one loftier and grander than that beneath it. The traveller's eye must come to rest somewhere in the end, either on the last and loftiest range as it stands silhouetted against the sky, or on the blue depths of haze, indistinguishable from the sky itself, into which the contours of ridge and peak melt and fade away. But the eye of the artist never comes to rest, for beauty is inexhaustible. She is the ever attained, and yet remains the ever unattainable, and therefore the artist's longing and desire for her, though perpetually satisfied, are perpetually unsatisfied, so that he presses eagerly on through keener satisfactions, diviner discontents, and intenser longings, until he realizes, if he had not realized it before, that the prize is in the race, and beauty in truth nothing but the rhythm of delight within his own experience.

Such is the natural egolessness of true artists, of the genuine devotees of Beauty, the sainted souls of Art. But here, just as we touch the highest point of our enquiry, two or three difficulties might arise, or one or two objections could be voiced, which must be resolved and answered before we can pursue the Religion of Art round into the full circle of its conclusion.

The first of these difficulties arises out of the apparent instability and irregularity which often distinguishes the lives of artists—poets, painters, and musicians—from the lives of non-artists. In the minds of most tax-paying, form-completing citizens art and immorality are almost synonyms, and it is more or less tacitly assumed that moral laxity is pre-requisite to artistic achievement. Though our contention that egolessness is the substance of art no less than of religion might be at least theoretically acceptable to such people, our assertion of its corollary, that the true artist, far from being immoral is, in fact, a spiritual being, and the genuinely aesthetic life essentially a life of spirituality would, therefore, probably appear in their eyes not only unacceptable but even positively absurd. Shrill voices would at once be raised to remind us of Byron's philanderings, while indignant fingers would point out to us the direction of Reading Goal.

The misconception out of which these difficulties arise is twofold. In the first place, it should not have passed unnoticed that, in our foregoing remarks, we have been careful to speak not of the artist—not just of any practitioner of poetry or painting, music or sculpture—but always of the *true* artist. What we intended this distinguishing epithet to convey has already been made partially clear by our fourfold classification of art into the (i) essentially as well as conventionally religious type, the (ii) essentially but not conventionally religious type, the (iii) conventionally but not essentially religious type, and the (iv) neither conventionally nor essentially religious type. As soon as it is realized that our subsequent definition of Art as *the organization of sensuous impressions into pleasurable formal relations that express the artist's sensibility and communicate to his audience a sense of values that can transform their lives* excludes the third and fourth types (which, as we had already hinted when discussing them, were not only not essentially religious, but even only superficially art) our conception of the true artist, as distinguished from the false practitioner of the arts, is one who produces art of the first and second types, that is to say, art which, either with or without the aid of accepted and understood religious symbols, communicates an experience which compels us to change our lives. As Carlyle finely says in *Heroes and Hero-Worship,*

> Poet and Prophet differ greatly in our loose modern notions of them. In some old languages, again, the titles are synonymous; *Vates* means both Prophet and Poet; and indeed at all times, Prophet and Poet, well understood, have much kindred of meaning. Fundamentally indeed they are still the same; in this most important respect especially, That they have penetrated both of them into the sacred mystery of the Universe; what Goethe calls 'the open secret'.[20]

What is here said of the poet is essentially true of the painter and musician, for Carlyle is really not concerned to point out the historical connection between the poetic and prophetic functions, so much as to vindicate the existence of a common spiritual element wherein both art and religion live and move and have their being. We believe that one who inhabits, as the true artist does, this spiritual element, who leads a life of egolessness by means of continual surrender to the incessant demands of the Beautiful, is hardly more liable to instabilities and irregularities of conduct than is that other swimmer in spiritual deep waters, the genuine saint, who leads a life of egolessness by unfailing surrender to the demands of the Good. This is not to say that the true artist may not sometimes behave egotistically; but this is due to the fact not that he is an artist but that he is a man, and constitutes a lapse from art no less than a fall from spirituality.

We believe that to the extent that he is faithful to Art he will be not only a truer artist than ordinary people but also much better as a man. That the lives of those who are not true artists, who produce art of the third and fourth types should, on the contrary, frequently be disfigured by intemperance or passional excess, is only what might have been expected, since it is but natural that the same lack of egolessness manifested by their art should also be exhibited in their lives. Moreover, just as in certain Shamanist rites (of a psychic rather than of a spiritual order) a state of trance can be induced in the celebrant by means of intoxicants, so in art which is not essentially religious (which stands in the same relation to true art as Shamanism does to true spirituality) a mood of seeming inspiration, or emotional excitation, can sometimes be induced by the abnormal stimulation of inordinate sensuous indulgence.

The difficulty of recognizing that the truly aesthetic life is also a life of spirituality arises in the second place out of a misconception of the nature of ethics. Those unbending moralists to whom art and immorality are practically synonymous terms are generally found adhering to an external and legalistic conception of morals. To them the moral life consists in the undeviating observance of an 'eternal and immutable' moral code, and this moral code is regarded not as a means to some sublimer spiritual end, but as being an end in itself. By its imperatives all human conduct is to be governed and judged: those who conform to them are moral, the salt of the earth, the elect of God; while those who can not or will not conform are immoral, accursed, and forever reprobate. We have no intention of questioning the utility of such prescribed patterns of behaviour. Neither society nor civilization could exist without them, and in the earlier stages of the spiritual life of the individual devotee they are indispensable. All we wish to point out is this, that however useful for practical purposes a moral code may be, the criterion of ethics is, nevertheless, fundamentally not external but internal. Although, generally speaking, a conventionally immoral action is at the same time an egoistic action, and therefore not only immoral but unspiritual as well, exceptional cases do occur which are conventionally immoral but in truth both egoless and spiritual. Sometimes it happens that a man may be compelled to shatter moralities out of the sheer intensity of his spiritual life. This is not antinomianism, for, as D. H. Lawrence has finely said, 'The true artist doesn't substitute immorality for morality. On the contrary, he *always* substitutes a finer morality for a grosser.'[21] The grosser immorality of which Lawrence speaks corresponds with the moral codes to which we have referred, and his finer morality to our life of egolessness and spirituality. Many spiritual masters appeared immoral in the eyes of their contemporaries because they had outgrown current notions of right and wrong. Socrates was sentenced to death for 'corrupting' the youth of Athens. Jesus was rebuked by the Pharisees for allowing his disciples to pluck ears of corn (which technically was 'working') on the Sabbath, and for setting them the example of eating with unwashed hands. The Buddha scandalized the orthodox brahmins of his day by disparaging the purifying power of ceremonial bathing, and by bluntly denying the value of animal sacrifices, both of which practices were then considered as being of the very essence of religion. All three masters were not behaving immorally but simply substituting a finer morality for a grosser one. Even while promulgating moral codes, both Jesus and the Buddha were careful to emphasize that such sets of rules possessed at the most a purely instrumental value: love of God and one's neighbour was the ultimate value for Jesus; to the Buddha, the realization of Nirvana.

We may therefore conclude that the widespread impression that art and immorality are practically synonymous terms has been produced by a combination of three causes: firstly, by a general failure to discriminate the true artist from the false; secondly, by the fact that, unlike the religious ascesis of the Buddhist devotee, the aesthetic ascesis of even the truest artist is rarely a conscious process, so that a fall from egolessness, and the consequent performance of an immoral action, is more to be expected of him than of his fellow-pilgrim on the parallel path of Goodness; and thirdly, by the fact that true artists, like genuine spiritual masters, do quite often substitute a finer morality of their own for the grosser moralities of the crowd. But in any case, there is no connection whatsoever between Art and immorality. All true Art in both essence and effect is egoless.

The remaining difficulty relates to the value of the Religion of Art not for the artist but to one who is simply a lover of works of art, whether in the form of poems or paintings, pottery or architecture, musical compositions or sculptures. Such people may possess a deep and genuine love of beauty, and may be keenly sensitive if not to all, at least to some of its numerous manifestations; but the necessity of earning a livelihood, the cramping pressure of daily rountine, and, above all, the exhausting strains and tensions of modern life, usually combine to prevent them from responding to the perceived beauty as actively and as ardently as they desire. Those to whom it is given to be saints of Art will always be a minority, even as among those who are called by religion few will be chosen as artists in the spiritual life. The major portion of any given human community is doomed by limitations of character, no less than by restrictions imposed through external circumstances, to stand not in the inner sanctuary of Egolessness but in its outer courts. As one might have expected, the predicament of the average art-lover runs almost exactly parallel to that of the ordinary religious-minded person. In the case of those who possess both artistic and religious interests, the parallelism is of course between twin aspects of their own personality. For whether one enters the temple of Egolessness by 'the gate which is called Beautiful', or through the portals of the Good, or whether one enters in by both simultaneously, the difficulty of how the average worshipper, with the dust of the world's roads still white upon his feet, can be enabled to participate, at least for a few moments, in the mysteries of the inner shrine remains the same.

The first step to be taken towards the resolution of this difficulty is to understand that between saint and sinner, artist and critic, creator and enjoyer, expert and amateur, there is a difference not of kind but only of degree. Just as there may be even in the true artist an element of egoism which sometimes makes him act like an ordinary mortal, so there is in the average man an element of egolessness which enables him upon occasions to experience Beauty as it is experienced by the true artist. With regard to their participation in egolessness through the mediation of the Beautiful the most devoted artist and the most casual enjoyer of works of art stand upon higher and lower rungs of the same golden ladder. With regard to the mode of their participation, however, there exists not a simple difference of degree but, at least from the point of view adopted at this stage of our enquiry, the far more radical difference of kind. The artist's participation in the Religion of Art is a predominantly active participation. He explores realms of experience before unknown, and reveals beauties hitherto unseen. The art-lover's participation, on the other hand, is passive rather than active. Not that active creation necessarily excludes passive enjoyment. All that we wish to point out is that whereas, in the artist's life, active participation in the Religion of Art by means of aesthetic creativity occupies a position of greater centrality than passive participation through mere enjoyment of works of art, in the experience of the art-lover the relative positions of these two modes of participation are reversed, and enjoyment predominates over creation. Once more an analogy between Art and Religion discloses itself. The relation between the creator and the enjoyer of a poem or statue is paralleled by that between the Master who gives and a disciple who receives a religious teaching.

'The Tathagata, brethren, who, being Arahant, is fully enlightened, he it is who doth cause a way to arise which had not arisen before: who doth bring about a way not brought about before: who doth proclaim a way not proclaimed before: who is the knower of a way, who understandeth a way, who is skilled in a way. And now, brethren, his disciples are wayfarers who follow after him. That, brethren, is the distinction, the specific feature which distinguishes the Tathagata who, being Arahant, is Fully Enlightened, from the brother who is freed by insight.'[22]

In these words does the Buddha contrast His own creative role in the drama of Buddhism with the comparatively passive part played by His followers. Since the ordinary person participates in the Religion of Art more as a disciple than as a Master, passively rather than actively, we shall deal with his enjoyment of the beauty of works of art first, and only afterwards with his own creation of beauty through personal aesthetic activity.

Beyond the very limited point to which merely untrained and instinctive appreciation of the fine arts suffices to carry him, the value of the Religion of Art to the average man depends upon the clarity with which he understands the distinction between false art which purveys the stale taste of ordinary egoistic human desire, and true art that caters to our deepest spiritual needs the rich and substantial diet, the unique savour, the unsurpassed relish, of emotions which, as they are without precedent in our experience, are an initiation into the mysteries of egolessness. This distinction between what may be provisionally termed 'good' and 'bad' art has to be made not so much for its theoretical value as for its practical consequences, just as in the religious life which parallels the life of art the distinction between ethically 'good' and 'bad' actions is drawn less for the satisfaction of the philosopher than for the guidance of the devotee. He who becomes a devotee of the Religion of Art is required to discriminate works of false art from works of art which are genuine not merely that he may understand but that he may eschew them. Just as the thief must stop stealing before he can become an honest man, and as it is necessary for the debauchee to abandon his impure line of conduct before he can become chaste, so is the renunciation of the enjoyment of bad art an indispensable prerequisite to the full enjoyment of good art. Egoism and egolessness are contradictory attitudes, and poems or pictures ensouling them cannot but inspire in the hearts of their 'enjoyers' emotions no less mutually contradictory than they are. Throughout the whole vast range of nature we see exemplified the law that when the great gods come the lesser gods depart. Unless the bud bursts the flower cannot unfold its petals, and unless the flower withers and dies in its turn no fruit can ever swell and ripen on the bough. In human life, too, childhood and adolescence, with all their charm, must pass away before maturity can be attained. Humanity must transcend itself in order to achieve super-humanity. Prince Siddhartha must die that a Buddha may be born. The Religion of Art's insistence that all pseudo-artistic rubbish must be swept from the highways of the soul before the car of Beauty can drive in triumph there is an application within its own domain of the same immutable law.

What practical difference does this prohibition make in the aesthetic life of the art-lover? If he accepts the authority of the Religion of Art, it will compel him to protect himself from bad art as carefully as he would take precautions against being infected by a particularly dangerous and virulent disease. He will have to stop reading almost all newspapers (which are generally bad literature in a state of putrefaction), pulp-magazines, and that vast mass of tenth rate fiction which the printing presses of the world turn out in such abundance. From second- and third-rate poetry, even, he should rigorously abstain, for although the quantity of first-rate poetry which has been written since the world began is small compared with that of other forms of literature, it is more than big enough to supply the utmost demands that may be made upon it by any single person. Cheap 'religious' lithographs, shoddy reproductions of popular paintings, and badly printed commercial calendars in all their gaudy hideousness, should be ruthlessly banished from the walls of his home. Inartistic furniture, carpets, curtains, and crockery should be dealt with in the same kind of way and replaced, if not by things which are genuinely beautiful, at least by articles which are well made, functionally appropriate, simple, and not so much an offence to the eye as such articles usually are. The devotee of the Religion of Art should be as much ashamed of being found with a sensational tabloid newspaper in his hand, a pair of unsightly factory-produced vases on his mantelshelf, or with two or three volumes of cheap fiction in his bookcase, as he would be if he was caught picking someone's pocket.

Turning from the contents of the home to the home itself, such a devotee should do his best to ensure that his house is as beautiful outside, in materials, structure, and setting, as it is inside. In this matter, the Indian peasant who lives in a thatched hut, with grey mud-plastered walls, cow-dunged courtyard and threshold ornamented with intricate designs in rice-paste, amid groves of plantain and mango, and with, perhaps, a pool or a tank nearby wherein to grow blue, red, or white lotuses, is more fortunate then the well-to-do city-dweller who lives in a house like thousands of other houses, in a street like thousands of other streets, with the smell of factory smoke in his nostrils and the noise of traffic thundering in his ears, with a balcony (if he is lucky!) or a grubby back yard instead of a garden, a compartment in a brick box instead of a home and, more likely than not, a bundle of nerves instead of a soul. In the countryside it is easy for a poor man to live beautifully, but in a city it is difficult even for a very wealthy person to do so. Things cannot escape from each other. Beauty and ugliness are both contagious; both spread and influence their surroundings. It is difficult for the city-dwelling art-lover to beautify his own house without beautifying the houses of his neighbours also, for their ugliness casts as it were a dark shadow over the beauty of his own abode. Similarly, ugly houses cannot be eschewed without rebelling against an ugly street, and a rebellion against an ugly street cannot succeed in a town given over to ugliness. It would seem as though the efforts made by the devotee of the Religion of Art to eschew bad works of art cannot be wholly successful without the co-operation of the entire community. Aristotle has said that the function of the state is to provide the conditions upon which the good life depends: it is no less the function of the state to assist its citizens to lead an aesthetic life. Offences against beauty are no less reprehensible than offences against morals, and hence no less deserving of punishment. A businessman who inflicts a hideous factory upon the skyline is as much a menace to society as an embezzler of public funds, and the architect who designed it, the contractor who built it, and the workmen who mixed the cement and swung the girders into position should be treated as his accomplices in crime. In a truly cultured community the unsightly buildings which disfigure most of our modern cities would not be tolerated for a day. Unfortunately, such communities have become rare almost to the point of extinction, and in the anguish of his soul the modern art-lover often thinks wistfully of the lovely cities of Ancient Greece, especially of Athens, city of the violet crown, with the Acropolis gleaming white upon her brow, and wonders whether Beauty will ever reign upon the earth as she reigned in those days over Hellas. Perhaps she will, if the Religion of Art succeeds in attracting a large enough following. Meanwhile, the art-lover, despite his inability to pull down ugly houses or re-plan unsightly streets, can at least eschew, within the walls of his own dwelling, false painting, literature, and music in at least some of their innumerable contemporary forms. Without taking this preliminary step, without cleansing his heart of the egoistically toned emotions which false art induces, deep and genuine appreciation of true art, together with all that such appreciation means for his spiritual life, will be impossible.

Before elucidating the significance of this appreciation, which will enable us to understand the value of the Religion of Art for its average devotee, we should briefly notice another form which, in modern civilization, the eschewal of ugliness often quite spontaneously takes: those periodical exoduses from town to country which seem to have become almost an institution in many Western lands. Even admitting that people who spend week-ends in the country or at the seaside are looking for health, amusement, or merely a change of scene as much as they are in search of natural beauty, still it cannot be denied that an unconscious urge to escape from the drabness and squalor of their everyday surroundings, and to gaze upon the face of a beauty untouched by man, impels them no less strongly than other motives. Unfortunately, as Aldous Huxley says in one of his earlier essays, 'Beauty-spots accessible to whole populations cease to be beauty-spots and become Blackpools'.[23] Regrettably true as this statement is, we are now concerned, not so much with appreciation of the beauty of Nature as one aspect of a modern social phenomenon, as with the place of that appreciation in the life of the average devotee of the Religion of Art. Kant points out the close connection between the aesthetic and religious aspects of existence, thereby indicating their common fundamental spirituality, when he says 'An interest in the beauty of nature for its own sake is always a sign of goodness.'[24] From our present standpoint the qualification 'for its own sake' is important. Since spirituality, or what the moralistically inclined Kant calls goodness, is, as we have seen, essentially an egoless attitude to life, there follows the consequence that only a selfless, that is to say a disinterested, appreciation of the beauties of nature is capable of expressing aesthetically the selflessness of the truly ethical character. In a passage on the love of flowers

D. H. Lawrence discriminates with remarkable insight between the interested and the disinterested appreciation of natural beauty.

> Now the love of flowers is a very misleading thing. Most women love flowers as possessions, and as trimmings. They can't look at a flower, and wonder a moment and pass on. If they see a flower that arrests their attention, they must at once pick it, pluck it. Possession! A possession! Something added on to *me*! And most of the so-called love of flowers today is merely this reaching out of possession and egoism; something I've *got;* something that embellishes *me.*
>
> Yet I've seen many a collier stand in his back garden looking down at a flower with that odd, remote sort of contemplation which shows a real awareness of the presence of beauty. It would not even be admiration, or joy, or delight, or any of these things which so often have a root in the possessive instinct. It would be a sort of contemplation; which shows the incipient artist.[25]

A sort of contemplation! Yes, and how unmistakably does Lawrence indicate the connection between Religion and Art, between the aesthetic and the ethical expressions of spirituality, when he makes this disinterested contemplation of a flower's beauty the sign of dawning artistic sensibility! Paradoxically, the value of natural beauty to the devotee of the Religion of Art is in inverse ratio to his merely egoistic consciousness that it has any value for him at all. The value of an inaccessible mountain peak, or of a serenely floating cloud, consists in its very valuelessness. It has no relevance to our material needs. We cannot turn the snow-clad peak into a human habitation, neither can we harness the white cloud to any earthly chariot. Nature is most beautiful when most aloof. Perhaps it is because of their sheer irrelevance to the needs of man, their utter indifference to his petty hopes and fears, that upon the face of gigantic mountain ranges, with their dreadful sunlit peaks and terrifyingly precipitous plunges into gloomy gorges, plays the intense and terrible light of a beauty never seen in fields or orchards, or in any other aspects of nature which have been brought in relation with the necessities of human life. Not that fields and orchards are unbeautiful. Formally speaking, they may be no less significant aesthetically than wilder and sterner scenes; but what the tabloid newspapers call 'human interest' generally obtrudes itself, like the moon between the earth and the sun in a solar eclipse, so that we see not the brightness of their beauty but only the dark shadow of their utility. For the same reason that he eschews bad art the art-lover would therefore be well advised, at least during the early years of his apprenticeship, to avoid the more domestic kind of natural beauty and to cultivate, instead, appreciation for those aspects of nature which, since they have no connection with ordinary human interests, are most capable of liberating him from the bondage of selfish desires. Egoism is natural to man, and to be overcome only with the utmost difficulty. Only too readily do we stop to pluck the flowers of the world's beauty, instead of wondering and passing on. A mountain, or a starry sky, offers no foothold to our desires. We are left as it were naked in the midst of a great empty space full of sweeping winds. Consequently, our enjoyment of their beauty is of the truly aesthetic order, and a faint anticipation of that intenser enjoyment to be offered us by the still brighter beauty of works of true art.

As we have already said, the artist's enjoyment of Beauty is more intense and active, while that of the *rasika* is less intense and comparatively passive. The artist is masculine, and plays the lover's role; the *rasika* is feminine, and assumes the part of the beloved. These differences will have to be borne in mind when assessing the value of the Religion of Art for the ordinary person, though, as we shall presently see in greater detail, they indicate not so much the presence of contradictory qualities as the predominance of one quality over another in a single individuality. Such differences apart, however, the value of the Religion of Art, for those who wait in its outer courts no less than for those who stand in the inner sanctuary, more than anything else consists in the broadening of their sympathies, in the enrichment and refinement of their experience, and in the uplifting of their transformed personality to new heights of being. Says Herbert Read:

> It has always been the function of art to stretch the mind some distance beyond the limits of the understanding. That 'distance beyond' may be spiritual or transcendental, or, perhaps, merely fantastical; somewhere it will overstep the limits of the rational.[26]

The distinction here made (rather diffidently, it seems) between the spiritual or transcendental, and the merely fantastical, aspects of the 'distance beyond' is, from the special viewpoint of the Religion of Art, without significance. If the fantastical does succeed in stretching the mind 'some distance beyond the limits of understanding', then the fantastical also is truly spiritual. For the presence of spirituality is revealed not by any outward sign but simply by that readiness to accept new experiences, that willingness to modify the pattern of one's existence, which is implied whenever we speak of transcending the limits of the understanding.

To us the most interesting and significant part of the passage quoted is the concrete and expressive term used to describe the relation of art to the mind. Art *stretches* the mind. . . How difficult it would be to find a more appropriate verb! It connotes a continuity, and, at the same time, a progressive development, of experience through higher and higher levels of subtilization not suggested by cruder and more abstract terms such as 'transcend', or even by concrete ones like 'overstep' and 'pass beyond', all of which imply that the mind is somehow lifted up bodily over the 'limits of the rational', like a small boy over a fence, and dumped down safely on the other side. The rational is not external to the mind, but the mind itself at one stage of its development, and to transcend the rational does not mean to transfer the mind unchanged from the rational to the super-rational plane (such transferals are possible only for physical bodies), but to continue changing it until a complete transformation takes place and it enters the super-rational stage of its development by becoming itself super-rational.

Time and again the literalness and abstractness of philosophic and religious terminology introduce confusions which vitiate the spiritual strivings of humanity. Most of these confusions, like that from which Herbert Read saves himself by speaking of stretching the mind, arise from the misconception that the mind, or soul, or whatever else it may be called, is not a flux, a process—a *santana,* as the expressive Pali word has it—in a state of continuous change and development, but an inert, unchanging *thing* subject only to external changes of time and place, and therefore differing from a stone in no observable particular. From this fatal misconception, which is in fact the rationalization of ordinary human egoism, the Religion of Art, no less than other forms of spiritual culture, promises to deliver us. If within the sphere of art itself the delusion that the mind is an immutable non-material 'substance' arises, the possibility of transforming the mind through art is precluded, and works of art are regarded not as engines of delight but solely as instruments of selfish pleasure, with the consequence that the pseudo-aesthetic life depicted by Tennyson in 'The Palace of Art', together with the ruin which inevitably overtakes such a life, of necessity ensues in place of the train of lofty consequences set in motion by the Religion of Art.

We should do well, therefore, to think of the function of art as being quite literally to stretch the mind (the implied comparison with a piece of elastic is far less objectionable than a covert comparison with a stone) further than the limits of its own rationality into the 'distance beyond' of Beauty, as this will enable us to see more clearly in what consists the value of the Religion of Art to its average devotee. Works of art are valuable to him because they stretch his mind. Usually, his mind is stiff and unyieldingly rigid; changes take place in it, but there is no development. The egoistic pattern of his life remains the same, though the elements composing it may vary from time to time. To a 'tough' mind like this, conventional religion nowadays often appeals in vain. Tug and pull as she may, it stubbornly refuses to be stretched or, even if she does succeed in stretching it for just a fraction of an inch, the minute her grip is relaxed it flies back to its former position more obstinately than ever. Then along comes the artist. Gently, very gently, he takes hold of the reluctant mind; slowly, oh so slowly, he starts drawing it out of itself, caressing and coaxing it all the time. Then, little by little, with infinite patience and inexorable firmness, he stretches and stretches it until it passes, no longer coarse and thick but delicate as the thread of a spider's web, over the limits of selfhood into that realm of selflessness which is the homeland of true art no less than of true religion.

At first the mind shrinks from the artist's touch; but it soon discovers that to be stretched is, after all, not such an unpleasant experience as it had supposed. Eventually, the experience becomes a positive delight, dearer, perhaps, and more rewarding, than any hitherto known. The spiritual life claims another devotee. So irresistible are the charms of Art. As Irwin Edman has written, 'Values translated into immediately loved images have a powerful suasion on the imagination'.[27] A single smile of Beauty can bring about greater transformations of character than all the frowns of Righteousness. Shelley gives fuller expression to the same idea when, in a famous passage of *A Defence of Poetry*, he declares:

> The great secret of morals is love; or a going out of our own nature, and an identification of ourselves with the beautiful which exists in thought, action, or person, not our own. A man, to be greatly good, must imagine intensely and comprehensively; he must put himself in the place of another and of many others; the pains and pleasures of his species must become his own. The great instrument of moral good is the imagination; and poetry administers to the effect by acting upon the cause. Poetry enlarges the circumference of the imagination by replenishing it with thoughts of ever new delight, which have the power of attracting and assimilating to their own nature all other thoughts, and which form new intervals and interstices whose void for ever craves fresh food. Poetry strengthens the faculty which is the organ of the moral nature of man, in the same manner as exercise strengthens a limb.[28]

What Shelley describes as a 'strengthening' of the mind corresponds to what Herbert Read speaks of as its 'stretching'. Despite dissimilarities—for illustrations do not agree in all particulars with their object, much less still with each other—both figures bring out an important fact. Just as a limb is strengthened, not merely during the period of exercise, but for the time when the exercise is no longer being performed, so the mind, even after being stretched by art beyond the limits of the rational, does not relapse into quite the same degree of rigidity as it was habituated to formerly. In plain language, the impression produced by looking at a painting, listening to a symphony, or reading a poem, does not disappear when we cease to look at the picture, or when the symphony ends, or when we put the poem by, or even when the memory of the delight they gave us has vanished, but remains a permanent part of our character modifying, in however slight a degree, the whole course of our life and conduct.

Since the experience of Art, like the experience of Religion, is essentially an experience of egolessness, the impression produced on the soul by the enjoyment of works of art will be of the same nature. The man who bears on his soul, as it were, the stamp of egolessness, whether derived from Religion through the will, or from Art by means of the imagination, will tend to act egolessly in all the relations of life. Such a one will be a good man in the noblest sense of the term, sensitive to the sufferings of others, sharing their sorrows and their joys, ready to help in time of need, not moved by 'greed or hate or fear', and ever seeking to share with his fellow men the joy of the Beauty which he has known. In this way, as Irwin Edman says,

> Aesthetic enjoyment and artistic creation are anticipations of what the Good Life would really be. Such happiness as is present among our contemporaries is the happiness of those who are doing work that is itself delightful to them and enjoying things that are themselves a delight.

The value to the ordinary man of participation in the Religion of Art through the enjoyment of beautiful things can be questioned only when the value of goodness, and the value of happiness, are questioned too.

The second way in which the average man participates in the Religion of Art is through his own creative activities. Here the difference between the saint and the devotee of Beauty is a simple difference of degree. All men have emotions; in fact, of such importance is the affective side of human life, that it might be more truthfully said that men are what their emotions are. Since emotion has a natural tendency towards self-expression, towards the creation, on the physical, aesthetic, or spiritual level, of an object in either its own likeness, or in the likeness of the thing, person, or event by which it was aroused, all men have a natural tendency towards the expression of emotion through creative activity. This expression may take two forms, one being achieved vicariously—for 'We are all poets when we read a poem well.'[30] —through the contemplation, the other personally through the actual creation, of works of art. Herbert Read clearly indicates the cathartic function of art when he writes

> The work of art is in some sense a liberation of the personality; normally our feelings are inhibited and repressed. We contemplate a work of art, and immediately there is a release; and not only a release—sympathy is a release of feelings—but also a heightening, a tautening, a sublimation.[31]

While not denying that this vertical release of feeling (as distinct from the horizontal release of mere sentimentality) can be effected by aesthetic contemplation as well as by aesthetic creation, we believe that the release effected through personal creative activity is generally more satisfactory and complete than any other. Probably most artists, poets, and musicians would agree with us. The average man, with whose needs we are now concerned, often discovers that his own artistic achievements, however clumsy and inept they may be, give him a strange feeling of satisfaction, a peculiar thrill of delight, such as he was never able to derive from the greatest works of art. Even a mud-pie, if he has made it with his own hands, may give a child more genuine pleasure than a costly painted toy. We therefore believe that, in much the same way as, for the religious devotee, vicarious attainment of sainthood by reading the lives of saints cannot make up for his own actual shortcomings, so even the widest and richest enjoyment of works of art will not be able to compensate the art-lover for the poverty of his own creative life.

Not that it is possible for any man to be absolutely uncreative, for then he would be totally lacking in emotive energy, and such a being would be an even greater freak than a man without a head. Our creative instinct is in fact generally more alive than we realize, and every day manifests itself in a hundred different ways. Dressing and adorning the body; furnishing a room; arranging books symmetrically on a shelf, or flowers in a bowl; planning a garden; laying the table for a meal; writing a letter; sewing a dress; embroidering a cushion; knitting a pullover; painting the woodwork of the house; making a kennel for the dog; icing a cake,—all these activities, and countless others, provide us with outlets for our creative energies. The more consciously and deliberately we make use of them, the greater will be the satisfaction they give us. Nevertheless they have their limitations. An ardent lover of Beauty will not be content with touching the fringe of her robe, but will want to lift up his eyes and behold her face. Such a person will feel surging within him energies too impetuous and vast to be confined within the narrow channels of the domestic creativity just described. He will long for a more quiveringly intense experience, a more purely ardent enjoyment; for that 'quintessential, keen, ethereal bliss' which, within the limits of the Religion of Art, only the actual creation of a work of art can give him. At first, his heightened creative activity may take the form, not only of combating ugliness in his surroundings—a subject which has been dealt with as preliminary to the enjoyment of works of art—but of trying to render them positively more beautiful. Sooner or later, however, he will feel compelled to start writing stories or poems, or to learn how to play a musical instrument, or how to paint or carve. Once he has reached this point, and begins creating works of art (however inferior or valueless they may seem in comparison with the productions of artistic genius) as well as enjoying them, he becomes a fully-fledged devotee of the Religion of Art, and worthy to stand, not merely in the outer courts of the temple of Beauty, but within the inner precincts and the secret shrine.

With the various kinds of creative activity, from poetry to pottery, or with the means whereby the skills necessary to the production of a work of art may be acquired, we shall make no attempt to deal. Information on these subjects is within the reach of those who really want it. Having briefly indicated the value of the Religion of Art to the average man, and having suggested ways in which he can deepen his participation in it through the enjoyment and creation of works of art, all that now remains to be done is to round off our remarks on the value of creative activities with two observations more, and then to conclude our enquiry into the Religion of Art with a few general reflections.

Enjoyment of an object is often enhanced by a sense of obstacles surmounted and difficulties overcome. In art, the difficulties and obstacles by which the artist is confronted are generally technical; they arise out of the intractability of his material, whether it be words, sounds, or pigments, out of the resistance it offers to the fiat of his creative will. The artist has to wrestle with his medium as Jacob with the Angel; but in the end it blesses him. One who knows naught of the struggle will not savour to the full the unction of that final benediction. This is the position of the man-in-the-Art Gallery, or in-the-library, or any other repository of finished works of art. He enjoys them mildly, like a cow in a field munching a daisy, for he knows nothing of the sweat which dropped from the giant thews of genius producing them; he knows nothing of the anguish of struggling with that which, while it is the greatest obstacle to the artist's achievement, is also the indispensable condition of his success; he knows nothing of the triumph of technique. The man-in-the-studio, on the other hand, the man who has at least tried to paint a picture or write a poem, knows from experience how difficult the task is, knows from his own bitter pains the problems of composition, the inexorable requirements of metre and rhyme. When he looks at a picture, or reads a poem, he will not only thrill with delight at beauties achieved, but rejoice at difficulties overcome. His enjoyment will be heightened and intensified to a degree that one ignorant of artistic technique will hardly be able to imagine. The actual creation of works of art is therefore of value to the average man, not only as an outlet for his emotional energies, but because it enhances his delight in the works of art produced by men whose genius is immeasurably superior to his own.

Inasmuch as men live not in solitude but as members of society, their activities and interests affect not merely themselves but others too. The value of the enjoyment and creation of works of art as outlets of emotional energies is not restricted to the individual artist or art-lover, but on the contrary possesses a significance which extends to the whole community. Emotion has a natural tendency to express itself. If it can find no outlet on the cultural level it will sink to the level of the physical and force an outlet there. Should opportunities for constructive expression be denied, then it will seize the first chance of expressing itself destructively. A child who is not encouraged to create will naturally learn to destroy. But destruction does not bring the same kind of joy as creation. After a few minutes of savage delight comes a reaction, a feeling of frustration sets in, and eventually the culprit feels even more miserable than he did before indulging in his bout of destructiveness. Many causes of juvenile delinquency and adolescent gangsterism are directly traceable to the fact that neither at home nor in school are sufficient outlets for the emotional energies of youth provided. For nearly all adults, the most frequently used outlet is the lowest and grossest, that of sexual intercourse.

Such an outlet the conventions of society quite rightly close to the young and unmarried. But society errs in providing for its younger members insufficient cultural and constructive means of releasing their emotional energies. Education generally places a stronger emphasis on the gaining of knowledge, or the acquisition of technical skills, than on the cultivation of the emotions. Art is certainly the Cinderella of education. Without going so far as to say that the intellectual and practical aspects of education are its Ugly Sisters, we do certainly wish to emphasize that if Cinderella is not allowed to go the ball she will not stay quietly at home washing the dishes; probably she will set the house on fire instead.

Though the problem of untrained emotion is acutest for adolescents, it is by no means absent from the life of adults (whose predominantly sexual solution is almost as big a confession of failure as the anti-social solution of wayward youth), and in fact is found in one form or another in practically every department of modern life. As Erich Heller's striking image reminds us, 'The workshops in which our truths are manufactured are surrounded by swarms of unemployed affections' and, as he goes on to warn us, 'Unemployment leads to riots'.[32] Not the smallest part of the value of the Religion of Art is that it restores our individual and social life to order by giving work to our unemployed affections, transforming them from not only lazy and yawning, but positively dangerous, drones into 'singing masons building roofs of gold'—the million-tiled golden roofs of the Temple of Beauty.

In these days, when, all over the world, conventional religion so often fails to move the hearts of men, the Religion of Art may enable some people at least to experience, through the instrumentality of Beauty, those supreme values of life which in former centuries were generally mediated by Religion. That in its present nascent condition the Religion of Art can mediate those values as fully and as effectively as the great historic faiths are even now able to do, we would not be justified in claiming. Whether in future it will ever be sufficiently developed so to mediate them, we hesitate to assert. But we believe that our enquiries have revealed no *a priori* reason why the Religion of Art should not be able, when consciously developed and utilized as a means of leading the spiritual life, the life of egolessness, to take for many people the place of religion; not, indeed, by becoming a Huxleian substitute, but through its mediation of those values which constitute the very life-blood of religion truly understood. Indeed, were the claims of the Religion of Art to be too invidiously weighed against those of conventional religion, in at least one respect the pan of the former would be found preponderating: the Religion of Art has never preached a holy war, or burned a heretic at the stake, whereas all religions except Buddhism have at one time or another been guilty of some form of persecution. History contains ample justification of Swift's celebrated aphorism that we have just enough religion to make us hate, but not enough to make us love, one another. May it never be said that the Religion of Art has ever tried to stifle the impulse of any noble soul!

Conventional religions may be organizationally strong, whereas the Religion of Art is organizationally weak; but their strength is their greatest weakness, while in its very weakness lies its greatest strength. The Religion of Art has no temple and no church; wherever men feel the touch of Beauty, there is holy ground. It possesses no scriptures; the whole of nature is its sacred book. It has no priests, for those who enjoy and those who create works of art behold Beauty face to face, and have no need of any mediator or intercessor. It has no membership, for the brotherhood of Beauty recognize each other at a glance; no fees, for her devotees are prepared to offer the sacrifice of their lives. By its very deficiencies, no less than because of its actual endowments, does the Religion of Art recommend itself to the hearts and minds of modern men and women. On account of its absolute freedom from institutional and credal bonds, as much as by reason of its irresistible appeal to all that is best and brightest in humanity, is it not only of supreme value to the constantly growing number of the creedless and unchurched, but also a useful supplement to the spiritual life of those who can still find in one established religion or another the main sources of their inspiration.

Deeply and firmly do we believe, that despite its present undeveloped condition the Religion of Art is peculiarly fitted to produce, in these troublous days, a kind of character, a type of spiritual personality, which will be the living embodiment of the fact that Religion and Art are in essence one, and that Beauty is not merely Truth, but Goodness as well.

Advice to a
Young Poet

Advice to a Young Poet

The utility of giving advice to a young poet may be questioned. One gives advice with the intention of improving, in some way or other, the person to whom it is addressed. Such a procedure may be admissible when we are concerned with an art or science that can be taught and learned; but with regard to poetry we have the assertion of Horace that poets are born, not made *(Poeta nascitur, non fit)*. Let us at the beginning of these remarks disclaim the fond hope that they will help make a poet out of anyone who is not a poet already. All that they hope to do is to tend what nature has planted; to suggest to the Young Poet ways in which the capacities he possesses may be developed; to indicate the discipline by which his still inchoate inspiration can be transformed into the deliberate creativity of the mature artist.

Poetry, like other things, has two distinguishable, though indivisible, aspects: substance and form. Our hints on the cultivation of these aspects will be given separately; but it should be borne in mind that the distinction is made for the sake of convenience in exposition, and does not correspond to any division of parts in the subject. In the fire of creative genius substance and form are made to coalesce into the partless whole which is a work of art.

By the substance of Poetry, we mean the experience that it contains. This experience is emotionally rather than intellectually toned; for although Poetry contains definite thoughts and ideas, in its essence it does not consist of these. Even the most abstract and philosophical statement possesses emotional value, however little that may be. Conversely, even the most intensely emotional poem contains intellectual elements. In the best poetry, however, these elements occupy a strictly subordinate place, and appear to function solely as aids to the exhibition of a non-intellectual experience. But here, too, we must beware of contrasting too sharply what are the co-existent aspects of Poetry rather than its mutually exclusive parts.

By the form of Poetry we mean the different species of poetic composition (lyric, epic, dramatic etc.), together with the various metres, stanza forms, and styles in which the predominantly emotional content is expressed. From our previous remarks it will be obvious without further explanation that the substance of Poetry is not related to its form as wax to a seal, but in a manner so intimate that it is strictly impossible to speak of a relation at all.

Poetry expresses the personality of the poet. It records his deepest feelings and sublimest thoughts, his tears and smiles, anguish and delight, frustration and fulfilment. In short it is the more or less complete embodiment of his whole experience of life. As the poet is, so also will his poetry be. Any change or development in the one will inevitably be paralleled in the other. To improve the poetry we must therefore, first of all, improve the poet whose expression it is. This improvement will not be ethical but artistic,—or at least not directly ethical; for, if Plato is to be believed, since Beauty, Truth, and Goodness are equally aspects of Reality, an approximation to one is also, indirectly, an approximation to each of the others.

The personality of the poet has, like the personalities of other men, two aspects: emotional and intellectual. The advice which we are about to offer the young poet therefore relates first of all more to the culture of his emotions, from which is created the substance of his poetry, and secondly more to the culture of his intellectual faculties, whence it derives its form. Once again, however, distinctions should not be mistaken for divisions. It should also be noted that the emotional and intellectual culture with regard to which our advice is offered is of a strictly limited kind, being simply what is significant and valuable from the poetic point of view. Moreover, our remarks are not exhaustive but suggestive. They do not provide a ready-made programme of poetic self-improvement, but simply point out some of the qualities which, in the writer's opinion, a young poet should take special pains to develop.

There are five predominantly emotional qualities—aspects of the poet's experience of life—which, when developed, will enrich the substance of his poetry. These are: Observation, Sensitiveness, Sympathy, Solitude, and Reflection.

All our knowledge and feeling begin from the impressions we derive from our five senses. Those derived from the eye, the organ of vision, are, however, more prominent and important than those entering through the ear or other senses, and we have, therefore, chosen the word *Observation* to cover the poet's intensified awareness of the whole external world. Everyone sees mountains, trees, flowers, houses, people's faces, and a thousand other things, every day. But the poet—or artist—should not be satisfied with merely seeing things: he must learn to observe them. Observation of course implies concentration. A poet should be prepared to spend a whole day looking at a flower, for only then will he be able to observe it. Observation means a vivid awareness of the unique individuality of things. A poet should be alive to the subtlest differences of colour, shape, contour, tone, touch, and smell, and should know the exactly right, the inevitable, word with which to describe every one of them. He should mark the different ways in which trees, in accordance with the stoutness or slenderness of their trunks and branches, and the relative scarcity or abundance of their leaves, dance and sway in the wind. He should be able to detect the change in the cuckoo's cry from month to month, while the personalities of different kinds of flowers should be as distinctly recognizable to him as those of individual human beings. This faculty of intense observation has been beautifully illustrated by Shelley, who says of the poet:

He can watch from dawn till gloom
The lake-reflected sun illume
The yellow bees in the ivy-bloom.

Incidentally, the description of bees as 'yellow' is a fine example of the kind of observation of which we are speaking. Any ordinary person, if asked to describe in one word the colour of a bee, would reply, either that it was brown, or that he had never noticed the insect's colour. The poets quite often startle us with epithets so fresh and original, yet withal so apt and vivid, that we realize with shame that we had never troubled to observe the objects to which their genius so triumphantly applies them. Those who are not poets can generally see nature much more vividly through the eyes of the poets than with their own. Who had really seen the blackness of ash-buds in March, or the greenness of the evening sky, until a Tennyson or a Coleridge had taught them to do so?

Second-hand observation may suffice for the ordinary person; but a poet cannot be satisfied with seeing nature through the eyes of another poet, however great. For him, in so far as he is a poet, not to see Nature with his own eyes is not to see her at all. Though he appreciates and admires the beauties of description found in poets of long ago, he does not simply purvey them at second-hand in his own poems. On the contrary, he observes Nature with his own eyes as clearly as he can, and describes what he has seen as strikingly as he is able. Few evidences of a decline in poetic vitality are more unmistakable than when poets slip into a habit of drawing their knowledge of natural objects not from life but from literature. Such bookish poets merely describe descriptions. Hence their poetry, though it may possess other great and noble qualities, does not impart to us the sensation of immediate impact with life. It may possess sweetness, artistry, and charm, but is lacking in freshness, vigour, and reality. Similes and metaphors, which are of the very essence of poetry, are born of personal observation. The more accurate and truthful is the poet's observation of the beauties of Nature, the readily will he apprehend the deeper relations and subtler interconnections which exist between them. The more ready this apprehension, the more original, impressive, and illuminating his similitudes will be.

By *Sensitiveness,* which is an entirely emotional quality, we mean depth and delicacy, or strength and refinement, of feeling. Most people consider those emotions to be powerful which are accompanied by violent physical action; but in fact the opposite of this belief is more nearly related to the family of truth. The more subtle an emotion grows, the less adequate become the normal bodily means of its expression. A blow or an embrace may suffice to embody the full content of the grosser forms of hatred and desire, but by what motions, save by those of poetry, music, and the visual arts shall the finer feelings of the human soul find expression? The poet is compelled to give vent to his emotions in verse because they cannot be realized through any human relation: they refuse to terminate, in the noble words of Plato, on finite and particular objects; but protract themselves into the infinite and universal realm of Poetry and Truth. It is in this capacity of protraction or penetration into Reality that the strength of an emotion truly consists. Subtlety and strength of feeling are, therefore, fundamentally one quality. This quality we have indicated by the term sensitiveness. The poet is aware of, and responds to, not only the grosser vibrations of the world of sense, but the immeasurably higher and finer vibrations of a world which lies beyond; a world which metaphysicians describe as a world of values, but which the poet generally prefers to describe as a world of ideal forms of Beauty. It should not be thought, however, that the poet's aspiration takes wing on a world-transcending flight of the alone to the Alone. If there be mysticism in poetry, it belongs more to the *via affirmativa* than to the *via negativa.* And if the poet possesses, as Aldous Huxley finely says of D. H. Lawrence (and his words have been applied with equal justice to Rainer Maria Rilke), 'a capacity of experiencing unknown modes of being', he experiences them not by abstracting himself from sensible objects, but rather by interpenetrating their essence with his own. Most poets would echo the words with which Wordsworth concludes his famous *Ode:*

To me the meanest flower that blows can give
Thoughts that do often lie too deep for tears.

The last words of these lines are significant. No outward and visible sign of emotion, such as tears, is capable of expressing the full depth of the inward and spiritual grace of the poet's thought, or the extreme intensity of his feelings.

Experience of this kind may be natural enough to a poet of Wordsworth's eminence, but by what means can the young poet of today even approach the altitudes at which they are possible? How is he to subtilize his feelings to the point at which they can become sensitive to the delicatest touches of the eternal beauty? The solution of this problem lies in the domain of what may be termed the asceticism of art. Aesthetic and religious experience belong to a common order, and in the former no less than the latter the higher and subtler reaches are to be attained by the renunciation of those which are, in comparison, low and gross. The philosophy of this ascesis, and the manner in which the lover of Beauty ascends from the experience of its lowest to the experience of its highest forms until, in the last supreme flight of his soul, he soars into the presence of Beauty Ineffable, has been for all time unfolded with matchless artistry in Plato's *Symposium,* wherein the incomparable genius of the Athenian poet-philosopher has magisterially blended the scattered rays of Philosophy, Religion, and Art into a single dazzling beam that penetrates far, far into the obscure depths of Reality.

In these remarks it is our more modest intention to offer only one or two suggestions (apart from advising the young poet to read and re-read the *Symposium*) concerning the cultivation of sensitiveness; for the subject is so intensely personal, and depends so much more upon the sincerity and integrity of the poet than upon the mechanical application of rules, that even these are advanced with hesitation. To begin with, it should be clearly understood that emotion is essentially a force, and that it has a natural tendency to express itself in some outward form. If this force is consciously checked, so that it is no longer able to express itself in the normal manner, the inhibited energy will assume a subtler and more powerful form, and therefore tend to find expressions on a higher plane of experience. Feelings are like fountains, in which the water, unable to find an outlet on its own level, shoots up through a narrow aperture to leap a hundred feet into the air.

It should be noted that the 'check' of which we speak is a conscious and deliberate process; were it unconscious, then the inhibited emotion would simply be pressed down beneath the conscious surface of the mind into the unconscious depths below, and what psychic disturbance a repressed emotion is capable of creating has been too strongly insisted on by psychoanalysts to need repetition here. The poet, like the mystic, has at all times to be aware of his feelings: he must saturate them with consciousness. For, like the breath, thought and emotion are naturally inhibited when the unwavering beam of awareness falls upon them, and at once resolve themselves into subtler forms, just as the dew melts, in the warm rays of the early morning sun, into the mist and air. These subtler forms are the raw material not only of art but also of spirituality. From them the poet, painter, and the musician create, in their respective media, images of imperishable beauty; while the mystic, repeating the process of inhibition over again, rises to even sublimer heights of experience. Such are the principles to be followed in the cultivation of Sensitiveness, or delicacy and depth of feeling. The exact manner of their application must be determined by the young poet, no less than by the novice in mysticism, for himself.

Supremely important as the cultivation of Sensitiveness is, it should not be supposed that in the previous paragraph we have advised the young poet to isolate himself in an ivory tower of rarified personal emotion. The varieties of Poetry are multitudinous, and by no means all of them deal with the poet's private feelings. Epic, narrative, and dramatic poems, for instance, are generally concerned with the thoughts, feelings, and actions of people far remote in time and place, and of widely different circumstances, from the poet who narrates them. Even lyric poetry, into which the poet's deepest and most intimate experiences naturally flow, is sometimes in a manner dramatic, being written by the poet not in his own character but in that of some other person, real or imagined. Here, however, our concern is not so much with the form as with the manner in which this is done. Descriptions must possess liveliness and poetic truth. It is not enough for the poet to observe accurately, and delineate naturally, the external effects of strong feelings; for as we have already said, such feelings cannot be adequately expressed by any bodily movements. By an act of sympathy he must project himself out of his personality into that of another being, and experience the emotions of that being because, for the moment at least, he has become one with him. This capacity for universal *Sympathy*, wherein the joys and sorrows of others are felt as keenly as our own, is yet another quality which has to be developed by the poet no less than by the religious devotee. The secret of art is identical with the secret of spirituality. Shelley writes in *A Defence of Poetry:*

> The great secret of morals is love; or a going out of our own nature, and an identification of ourselves with the beautiful which exists in thought, action, or person, not our own. A man, to be greatly good, must imagine intensely and comprehensively; he must put himself in the place of another and of many others; the pains and pleasures of his species must become his own.

The emotion to which Shelley, in this passage, from his more general point of view, has given the name 'love', corresponds with what we, from the special point of view of Poetry, have called 'sympathy'. We would go further than Shelley only in advising the young poet not merely to make the pleasure and pains of the human species his own, but to cultivate a feeling of identity with, and sympathy for, every kind of sentient being. '. . . If a Sparrow come before my Window I take part in its existence and peck about in the gravel', wrote Keats in one of his letters. The poet's sympathies must be universal. He must be able to enter into the existences, and share the feelings, not only of human beings, not only of birds and beasts, but even of trees, flowers, mountains, streams, and stones. A poet in whom this quality of sympathy is highly developed will be able to describe the thoughts and emotions of others with peculiar force and vividness. For he will be describing not what he has observed from without but what he has experienced from within.

It is for this reason that supreme Poetry, no less than the higher kind of Religion, possesses the capacity to lift us out of the littleness of our individual being into an infinitely deeper, richer, and wider kind of life. To read poetry of this exalted type is much more than witnessing unfamiliar situations and novel sentiments: it is an initiation into a new mode of being. Momentarily we experience what the poet experienced when with his 'glassy essence' he interpenetrated the essence of another form of life and felt the pulsation of its existence as his own. Sympathy is therefore closely allied to self-transcendence, to the power of getting beyond one's personal ego.

A self-centred man may be a competent versifier; but he can never be a great poet. Beauty and goodness once more join hands. The cultivation of sympathy implies the adoption of a selfless attitude towards life. As remarked at the beginning of these suggestions, we entertain no hope that they will be able to make a poet of anyone who is not a poet already. The utmost they can accomplish is to help in the development of a congenial aptitude. Sympathy, even more, perhaps, than any of the qualities already mentioned, is a natural endowment; and we are therefore able to offer less advice on its cultivation than on that of any other quality. All that can be suggested in this regard is that the cultivation of observation and sensitiveness will naturally contribute to the enlargement of the poet's sympathies. Since we generally find it easier to sympathize with the sorrows than the joys of our fellow men, the young poet may in addition be recommended to direct his attention first of all to the miseries and misfortunes of others, and only afterwards to their consolations and blessings. For if they are contemplated in reverse order, he may feel not sympathy but envy. More than this cannot be said on the subject without trespassing beyond the uncertain boundary which divides the life aesthetic from the life spiritual, and exchanging the realm of Poetry for the sister realm of Religion.

The qualities which the young poet should develop are not only interrelated, so that the cultivation of one leads indirectly to the cultivation of others, but they are also linked serially, so that each springs naturally into existence out of the very abundance of the quality preceding it. Observation flowers into Sensitiveness, and Sensitiveness ripens into Sympathy. The mind of the young poet is at this stage replete with vivid impressions of forms and colour; his heart responds immediately to the subtlest nuances of feelings; the horizons of his soul have widened until he can begin to say, with Sir Edwin Arnold, 'Forgoing self, the universe grows I'. But, before the work of poetic creation can begin, the richly diverse products of these three qualities must be mingled and fused as elements are fused in a crucible, the dross of irrelevancies purged from them by fire, and the imperishable poetic essence extracted. The crucible is *Solitude;* the fire *Reflection*.

Without some degree of solitude reflection is impossible, and without prolonged reflection no great work of art was ever brought forth. The poet needs solitude as the lungs need air. By Solitude is meant not so much physical loneliness as inner isolation, for the time being at least, from all that does not directly concern the process of poetic creation. Physical withdrawal from normal human activities and interests can be included in the definition of solitude only to the extent that the latter is dependent on it. In the urbanized and industrialized societies of the present age this is with increasing frequency the case. Without withdrawing externally form the hurry and bustle of modern life the poet may not be able to find the internal solitude necessary for the progress and perfection of his work. At the same time, the necessity of earning his own livelihood—on its own level a no less urgent problem—again and again draws him from solitude back into society. In a world wherein Poetry as a profession is no longer recognized or remunerated, the young poet has to find a way of life which will enable him to provide for both the lower and higher necessities of his nature.

The religious mystic, to whom opportunities for solitude are as necessary as to the poet, can find them in the solemn hush of monastery or hermitage; but corresponding facilities are not offered by an indulgent society to the poet. Perhaps it is just as well they are not. Opportunities for sympathy are no less precious or necessary to him than opportunities for solitude, and it cannot be denied that through the complex network of mutual ties and obligations woven in the course of earning a livelihood they are most easily and naturally secured. Having already refused to allow Sensitiveness to open for the young poet the portals of the ivory tower, it would be strange if we permitted Solitude to usher him through them. The kind of solution which we envisage should be neither unbalanced nor one-sided: it should exemplify poetically what Baron von Hügel said of the spiritual life: 'The great rule is, *Variety up to the verge of dissipation: Recollection to the verge of emptiness*: each alternating with the other and making a rich fruitful tension'.

The extremes of variety and recollection, dissipation and emptiness, of which von Hügel speaks, correspond with the extremes of sympathy and solitude between which the young poet has to pursue a middle path, and for both of which we have urged him to provide opportunities in his life. As circumstances will tend to force him into the first extreme, and as opportunities for solitude are in modern times the rarer of the two, we shall, however, consider the problem from one side only and, after enunciating a general rule, put forward a few more detailed suggestions with regard to the cultivation of solitude.

The general rule is negative in form, and consists in the simple reminder that the young poet should not embrace any means of earning his living which does not grant him regular periods of respite from its preoccupations. The longer and more frequent such periods, the more congenial the employment will generally be to him. Prospects of financial gain (above what is actually needed for the maintenance of himself and his dependents, if any), hopes of worldly advancement, and consideration of social prestige, must the poet no less than the contemplative brush resolutely aside. The temptation of commercializing his literary gifts must be no less uncompromisingly resisted. This is not to say that he should refuse to accept payment for his work; for in this field, as in any other, the labourer is worthy of his hire. But the poet should not resort for his livelihood to journalism, or to the production of novels, short stories, and newspaper articles from motives predominantly commercial. Should he prostitute his talent in this way he will eventually lose even his poetic integrity. He cannot divide his literary character into two separate personalities. The more money he needs, the more work he is compelled to produce; the more he produces (beyond a certain point), the more slipshod it becomes; slipshod work results in a general lowering of standards and this, in the end, will vitiate even the quality of his poetry.

If a young poet desires an avocation which, while not unconnected with his literary interests, will nevertheless involve no degradation of his art, he perhaps cannot do better than adopt an academic career, and teach languages and literature, history, or some other humane subject. Otherwise, farming or bricklaying is preferable to journalism. For it should not be thought that a poet is necessarily unfit for manual labour, or incapable of practical activity of any kind, or that the sensitiveness of his heart has in any degree impaired the dexterity and usefulness of his hands. The annals of Poetry are no more wanting in the names of politicians, statesmen, administrators, engravers, apothecaries, ploughmen, doctors, and traders, than in the names of writers and teachers.

Matthew Arnold's famous description of Shelley as 'a beautiful but ineffectual angel' is applicable to no other poet of equal stature, and is less than fair to Shelley himself. The popular picture of the poet as a long-haired, effeminate, and incompetent creature was never more than a late nineteenth century caricature of a group of minor poets, and is now less true than it ever was. There is nothing in the poet's constitution to prevent him swinging a pick or handling a shovel, and such a means of livelihood may be, for some, no less conducive to the pursuit of Poetry than any other. The sole question which the young poet, as such, has to ask himself regarding any form of employment is: Does it give me opportunities for solitude? If it does, he can, as a poet, ask of it nothing more.

It should not be thought, however, that the suggestions we have offered are an infallible and universally applicable solution of the problem of solitude. The poetic temperament is rarely amenable to the rules of reason. Even though the young poet succeeds in finding work which provides him with opportunities of withdrawal from the world, of experiencing those periods of inner isolation so necessary to the progress of his work, he may find that his creative moods refuse to synchronize with office hours or college vacations; that just when his whole being cries out to be alone, to be free to concentrate on the shaping of a poem, some trivial detail of the daily round claims his attention.

Contrariwise, he may spend weeks and months in apparently ideal surroundings and yet feel his heart as dry as dust and his soul incapable of producing even the thinnest trickle of inspiration. The wind of Poetry, like other winds of spirit, bloweth where it listeth. Again, there are social obligations and family ties to be considered. Like the mystic, the poet has often felt them to be a hindrance; and like the mystic, he has often not hesitated to snap them when they have become too restricting. The mystic's renunciation of such obligations and ties is usually recognized and approved by society; but the poet's repudiation, being much more haphazard and unsystematic, is usually considered as evidence of a disposition to immorality. Though, as D. H. Lawrence says, 'The true artist [or poet] doesn't substitute immorality for morality. On the contrary, he *always* substitutes a finer morality for a grosser'. To all these problems we can offer no cut-and-dried solution. All that we can do is to reiterate the necessity for solitude, and leave the young poet to make provision for it, in the light of our suggestions, as amply as he can.

Once the crucible has been prepared, the fire may be kindled beneath it. When the poet finds himself in solitude, in conditions favourable to the cultivation of inner isolation, the process of *Reflection*, of extracting the shining gold of poetry from the drossy ore of experience, can begin. About this process we need say little. Not that it is unimportant, though. Bagehot indicates its position when he writes, 'One of the reasons for the rarity of great imaginative art is that in very few cases is this capacity for musing solitude combined with that of observing mankind'; And Wordsworth does likewise in his famous definition of Poetry as 'Emotion recollected in tranquillity'. The word 'musing' in the first quotation, and 'recollection' in the second, both refer to the process which we have termed Reflection. If we have less to say about this quality than the four preceding ones, it is not, therefore, because of its relative insignificance, but because of the obscurity and mysteriousness of this part of the poetic process. How, from his experience of life, from his observations, feelings, and thoughts, he produces, like the musician, 'not a fourth note, but a star', is known only to the poet himself, and even he is rarely able to offer an adequate description of the process, to say nothing of giving an explanation of it which will satisfy the philosopher. His definitions and descriptions are usually figurative, and more often than not in the end themselves become poems.

It will therefore hardly be an occasion for surprise if the few words of advice which we intend to offer the young poet on the cultivation of reflection are figurative rather than scientific in character. The fire of reflection must be kindled as often, and kept burning for as long, as possible. In one who is by vocation a poet this flame of slow quiet musing is always present, however deeply it may be hidden under the ashes of external activities and events, and only waiting for the breeze of solitude to fan it into a blaze. This sacred fire of reflection must the young poet learn to tend as carefully as though he was a Zoroastrian priest, feeding it with the sandalwood of his thoughts, and stirring the ore of his experience in the crucible of inner isolation until the fine gold of Poetry, separated from the dross of irrelevant circumstances, glitters at the bottom like a star.

Having offered our suggestions on the cultivation of the five predominantly emotional qualities which will enrich the content of his poetry, we shall now suggest to the young poet three predominantly intellectual acquisitions which will help give precision and definition to its form. None of these may be adequately designated by any single word; but they may be provisionally indicated by the terms Appreciation, Understanding, and Technique.

The word 'poet' means, literally, a maker, and like all other makers or craftsmen the poet has to undergo a period of apprenticeship to those more skilled than himself in the gentle craft which he aspires to master. During this period of training he learns to know and appreciate the work of his predecessors. This *Appreciation* is not a mere spark produced by the cold collision of the flint and steel of criticism, but a flame begotten on the tinder of his heart by the fiery seed of their greatness. Neither is it mere imitation. It does not, or should not, teach him the mannerisms, however magnificent, or tricks of style, however effective, of 'poets dead and gone'. The chief function it has to perform is to fan into brightness the flame of his poetry with the mighty breath of inspiration which blows through their song.

Nor should it be thought that this breath can come only through the mouth of his native language. In these days of close international contact, if not always of co-operation, the poet, no less than other men, has to keep himself open to the impact of multitudinous influences. The English poet, for instance, must learn to appreciate, at least in translation, the best poetic work which has been done not only in French, German, and Italian, but also in Arabic, Persian, and Chinese. No non-English poet, on the other hand, especially if he is working in one of the undeveloped minor languages of the world, can afford to neglect the unequalled riches of English poetry. Such a commerce between the languages and literatures, but especially the poetic literatures of many times and lands, will contribute to the growth of a newer and more truly international kind of Poetry which will embody the ideals and aspirations, not of any single race or people, but of humanity.

Though we have spoken only of Poetry, it should not be thought that we are implying any limitations on the young poet's appreciation to the progeny of his own peculiar Muse. The daughters of Clio and Euterpe must be as dear to him as the sons of Calliope and Erato. Without suggesting that every poet should attempt to follow in the footsteps of Blake and Rossetti—for the mastery of two arts is more than twice as difficult as the mastery of one—it should at least be pointed out that the scope of Poetry is often considerably enlarged when the poet is familiar, not with Poetry alone, but with the sister arts of Music and Painting as well. Poetry is a limpid mountain lake into which flow the streams of every branch of knowledge and invention. The greater the volume of such tributary waters that it receives, the deeper and fuller will its own waters become.

Among the many streams which feed the tarn of Poetry is that of Philosophy. Not that an academically adequate acquaintance with the subject is essential to a poet. But of the course of that particular channel by which they are connected, he should have at least some knowledge. This channel is the philosophy of Art, or Aesthetics. Familiarity with the Philosophy of Beauty on the theoretical side will not ensure that his poetic work will be beautiful; but it will help give him an intellectual understanding of the metaphysical nature of Poetry, and this *Understanding,* the second of the intellectual qualifications with which the young poet should be equipped, will strengthen the structure of his verse, and while it is incapable of making him a good poet, may be able, by sharpening his faculty of self-criticism, at least to prevent him from being a very bad one.

Not much more than this can be said of the third qualification, that of Technique, which consists in a working acquaintance with the details of Rhetoric and Prosody such as may be found in standard manuals on the subject. Such acquaintance may not be sufficient to set the young poet's heart on fire with the flame of inspiration; but it will at least enable him to be sure that the fuel is dry. Though the shortest, this is not necessarily the least valuable part of the advice we have endeavoured to offer those who have apprenticed themselves to one of the most difficult and delightful of arts.

Paradox and Poetry in The Voice of the Silence

Paradox and Poetry in *The Voice of the Silence*

Buddhist canonical literature, which subsists not merely in volumes but in libraries, falls quite naturally into two main groups, each possessing certain distinctive features. The sutras, as the works comprising the first and more important group are designated, purport to be discourses delivered by the Lord Buddha Himself or, in a few cases, those given by Arahant and Bodhisattva disciples speaking either with His approval or under His inspiration. The sastras, the works comprising the second group, are treatises composed by the great *ācāryas,* founders and exponents of the various Buddhist schools, in order to elucidate and systematize the teachings of a particular sutra or group of sutras. The distinctive features of these two groups of works, which we have differentiated at length elsewhere,[1] will for our present purpose be sufficiently indicated by saying that whereas the method of the sutras is direct and intuitional, aiming at spiritual awakening rather than intellectual conviction, that of the sastras is definitely more discursive and logical.

The Voice of the Silence, though it does not claim to be the utterance of a Buddha, is nevertheless akin to the sutra rather than to the sastra group of texts. Like the longer and more celebrated discourses, it seeks more to inspire than to instruct, appeals to the heart rather than to the head. To make use of De Quincey's classification, it belongs not to the literature of information, the purpose of which is to augment knowledge, but to the literature of power, the aim of which is to move. So important is a clear understanding of the difference not merely between the kinds of effect they are calculated to produce and the organs upon which they are intended to act that, according to *The Voice of the Silence* itself, the disciple at the very outset of his quest is admonished, 'Learn above all to separate Head-learning from Soul-wisdom, the "Eye" from the "Heart" doctrine'.[2] By Head-learning is meant, of course, a merely intellectual understanding of spiritual truths. Not that such an understanding is deprecated, much less still condemned: the Master simply insists on the necessity of recognizing its limitations, a task which most people—even religious people—seem to find extremely hard. Soul-wisdom on the other hand signifies what the *Prajñāpāramitā* corpus of sutras calls simply *prajñā*, Wisdom, and the *Laṅkāvatāra Sūtra āryajñāna*, Noble Knowledge, a purely transcendental faculty for the apprehension of spiritual truths which, when fully developed, is identical with the Bodhi or Enlightenment of a Buddha. Just as it is the function of the 'Eye' doctrine of the sastras to impart Head-learning, so it is the function of the 'Heart' doctrine of the sutras to stimulate the development of Soul-wisdom. We are not to suppose, however, that there are two doctrines, in the sense of two different bodies of teachings: it is a question of a difference of attitude, of approach. Inasmuch as it conforms to the sutra rather than to the sastra type of literature, *The Voice of Silence* seeks to awaken Wisdom by appealing to the heart—not a physical organ but a transcendental faculty—and by encouraging the disciple to adopt an attitude in which the intellectual will be subordinated to the spiritual.

How does it do this?

Buddhism, it is well known, upholds the equal validity of reason (*anumāna*) and experience (*pratyaksha*). The latter is twofold, consisting on the one hand of the contact of the five sense-organs and the mind (regarded as merely a sixth sense) with their respective objects, and on the other of the various levels of *dhyāna* or *samādhi* wherein, though consciousness is intensified, the senses and the mind no longer function. This second type of experience is itself subject to further subdivision. If the object of the *dhyāna* or *samādhi* is, though good (*kusala*), still mundane (*laukika*), the experience itself, despite the fact that it transcends the physical and mental levels, is necessarily mundane too, and as such incapable of directly conducing to liberation (*moksha*). If the object of the *dhyāna* or *samādhi* is transcendental (*lokuttara*) the *dhyāna* or *samādhi* is also transcendental and its development therefore equivalent to the attainment of a stage of the Transcendental Path leading directly to Nirvana.

This distinction between the two types of meditational experience, one mundane, the other transcendental, is of the utmost importance, and had it been more widely known and uncompromisingly insisted upon, the world would have been less at the mercy of teachings which, though claiming to issue from the Absolute, in fact proceeded only from the upper reaches of the phenomenal. Whether transcendental or mundane, however, *samādhi* in the full sense involves not only a holding of the senses in abeyance but also a complete suspension of mental activity, and it is perhaps this very fact which, by acting as an occasion for a misapplication of the principle of the identity of indiscernibles, has been chiefly responsible for the confusion of these two radically different modes of experience.

Since in *samādhi* the mind is transcended, it follows that the various functions of the mind, such as perception, memory, and ratiocination, are transcended too. Consequently, the possibility of giving an account of *samādhi*, in terms of the concepts which the mind has either generalized from sense-impressions or evolved spider-like from its own entrails, is by the very nature of the meditational experience precluded.

The superconscious, as the mystics of all religions have insisted, is beyond reason. This does not mean that it contradicts reason. For it could contradict reason only if they occupied a common level; if it diverged from reason as it were on the horizontal plane, instead of being separated from it, as with the mundane *samādhi*, vertically, or as with the transcendental *samādhi*, by the abrupt disappearance of the latter into a 'fourth' dimension which, since it is transcendental hence absolute, stands in no relation to reason at all. Only reason can contradict reason. In fact, as Nagarjuna and his followers maintained, reason is inherently self-contradictory. We should therefore be on our guard against the very common error of assuming that by the mystical is meant anything irrational and illogical. As T. S. Eliot sardonically remarks, before one can go beyond the intellect one must have an intellect.

But meanwhile the problem of communication remains. How is it possible to convey the nature of *samādhi* to one who has no personal experience of it when language, the main vehicle of communication, is derived from those very levels of experience which *samādhi* transcends? Certain Zen masters, of course, solve the problem in their own way by endeavouring to dispense with language altogether. The traditional Buddhist solution of the problem is much less drastic. One group of sutras, of which those constituting the *Prajñāpāramitā* corpus are the most prominent, places its reliance mainly on the method of systematic paradox. Another group, which includes the *Saddharma Puṇḍarīka* and the *Larger* and *Smaller Sukhāvatī-vyūha Sūtras*, has recourse to poetry, especially in the highly developed form of cosmic myth.[3] *The Voice of the Silence* is probably unique in making use of a combination of both methods, a procedure which no doubt has much to do with the extraordinary effectiveness of this little treatise in awakening the dormant Soul-wisdom of the qualified disciple. Before proceeding to illustrate this thesis with examples from the text itself it will be necessary for us to try to gain a clearer understanding of the nature of both paradox and poetry.

A paradox has been facetiously defined as a truth standing on its head to attract attention. As far as it goes the definition is not a bad one, for in its own way it does attempt to bring out two highly relevant points: firstly, that a paradox involves a contradiction and, secondly, that it contains an element of truth. In the case of a paradox in the merely rhetorical sense of the term the contradiction is only apparent and the truth which it is intended to emphasize quite capable of being stated logically: the paradoxical form is no more than a literary trick to excite attention. The paradoxes of the Buddhist scriptures, however, are what may be termed paradoxes *per se;* the contradictions they involve are real contradictions, and the truths which, through those contradictions, they try to convey, or better to indicate, are truths not susceptible to logical analysis. Buddhist paradox, in other words, is an attempt to express in terms of logical contradiction that which transcends logic. Exactly how this is done cannot be understood without at least passing reference to the so-called Laws of Thought.

According to the first of these, the Law of Identity, A is A, which means that it cannot be not-A, or that a thing is identical with itself. The second law, the Law of Contradiction, states that A is not not-A. The third, the Law of Excluded Middle, states that A either is or is not B; meaning that between two contradictory statements there is no middle ground, so that if one is denied the other must be affirmed. These laws or principles of thought constitute, at least in theory, the ultimate foundation not only of all philosophy but of every field of human achievement in the development of which reason has played a part, and to deny them at that level would produce on civilization and culture an effect comparable to that of a violent earthquake upon a town. So disastrous a denial as this is never contemplated, of course, by the genuine mystics (who usually display sterling common sense in their attitude to the affairs of everyday life) for, as the Mahayana so emphatically maintains, the absolute truth is not to be realized except in dependence on the relative truth. But whatever their other differences may be, probably all mystics without exception refuse to commit what would be for them the elementary mistake of trying to abide by the Laws of Thought when speaking of those things which transcend logic because they transcend the rational mind. Spiritual experience, they unanimously insist, is as it were three-dimensional, the intellect two-dimensional. Even as a number of 'contradictory' projections of a portion of the globe can give us, when compared, a more adequate idea of its true size, shape, and contours than only one, so a statement which involves a logical contradiction stands a better chance of being able to describe the content of the *dhyāna-samādhi* experience than one which is logically self-consistent.

For this reason do the religious geniuses of all times and ages, attempting to describe the indescribable, speak of the dark light, the dazzling darkness, the nothing which is everything, the voidness which is full. Hence, admonishing the spiritual aspirant, do they urge him to lose his life in order to find it. In all these paradoxes, though, expressive and effective as they are, lurks still some residue of the merely literary and rhetorical. Only in the Buddhist sutras, perhaps, especially in those of the *Prajñāpāramitā* corpus, can we find the paradox of unmitigated logical contradiction in all its glory employed on a grand scale to express the experiences not merely of mundane *samādhi* but of the transcendental.

Says the *Vajracchedikā Sūtra*, describing the attitude to be developed by the Bodhisattva:

> One who has set out on the career of a Bodhisattva should reflect in such a wise: 'As many beings as there are in the universe of beings, comprehended under the term "beings",—eggborn, or born from a womb, or moisture born, or miraculously born, with or without form, with perception, without perception, with neither perception nor non-perception,—as far as any conceivable universe of beings is conceived; all these I should lead to Nirvana, into the realm of Nirvana which leaves nothing behind. But, although innumerable beings have thus been led to Nirvana, no being at all has been led to Nirvana. And why? If in a Bodhisattva the perception of a 'being' should take place he would not be called a 'Bodhi-being'. He is not to be called a 'Bodhi-being' in whom the perception of a self should take place, or the perception of a being, or the perception of a living soul, or the perception of a Person.[4]

This boldly paradoxical passage makes it clear that since he has his being in a sphere describable only in terms of logical contradiction, the Bodhisattva, as he manifests in the world of the senses and the mind, is himself a contradiction, a living paradox.

Even more tersely explicative of the *Prajñāpāramitā's* 'logic of contradiction' is a text from the *Saptaśatika* in which the Buddha says:

> ' "Beings, beings", O Subhuti, as non-beings have they been taught by the Tathagata. Therefore are they called "beings" '.[5]

Greater havoc could hardly be played with the Laws of Thought than this!

The Voice of the Silence uses paradox as a method of awakening Soul-wisdom in much the same way as the *Prajñāpāramitā*, though of course it does not use it on nearly so grand a scale. Even the title of these chosen fragments from 'The Book of the Golden Precepts' is, as a moment's reflection will show, profoundly paradoxical. It is as though the hand which transcribed them for the good of humanity, and dedicated them 'To the Few', had written in letters of fire above the sanctuary portal an awful warning that here was ground upon which the intellect could not tread, where only a chastened and sublimated spiritual intuition that worked not within the narrow bounds of formal logic could possibly hope to gain admittance. May that warning not go unheeded as we attempt to bring to the surface a few of the pearls of meaning which lie hidden in the abyss of this paradoxical juxtaposition of the contradictory terms 'Voice' and 'Silence'.

Mme. Guyon, the great 17th century French mystic who was the friend and spiritual adviser of Fenelon, makes a distinction which will be of use to us in approaching our subject. There are, she says, four kinds of silence: the silence of sound, the silence of desires, the silence of thoughts, and the silence of the will. These are of course not unknown to Buddhist tradition. In the *Saṁyutta-Nikāya* of the Pali *Sutta-Piṭaka*, for example, occurs a passage which makes it perfectly clear that the *ariya-mona* or 'noble silence' of the Buddhist texts corresponds to the third of Mme. Guyon's four silences (not to the first, the silence of sound, as generally imagined). After relating to the brethren how, when he was secluded and living all alone, there had occurred to him the discursive thought 'The Ariyan silence! they say. Now what means this Ariyan silence?' Moggallana the Great, one of the two Chief Disciples of the Buddha, proceeds:

'Then, friends, I thus thought: "Herein a brother, by the suppression of discursive thought and investigation, enters on and abides in the Second Trance, a state of

> internal calm of heart, concentrated on its object, free from discursive thought and investigation, born of mental balance, a state of zest and ease. This is called the Ariyan silence." '[6]

Here *ariya-mona* is plainly equated with the second *jhāna* (Skt. *dhyāna*), wherein, in contradistinction to the first *jhāna*, there is no discursive thought and investigation (*vitakka-vicāra*) but only concentration (*samādhi*), zest or joy (*pīti*), and happiness or ease (*sukha*).

More germane to our present enquiry, however, is the fourth kind of silence, the silence of the will. By will Mme. Guyon presumably understood self-will, that is to say, any movement of the soul that was not in accordance with the will of God. So much must the will of the creature be one with that of the Creator that, according to her doctrine of disinterested love, the soul must love God even though he decrees its damnation. Obviously the conception of will is closely linked with that of self. In a sense they are correlative. If the one is grossly conceived, the other will be grossly conceived too; if subtly, with corresponding subtlety. Immured as she was within the Christian tradition, Mme. Guyon, for all her acuteness, could hardly be expected to perceive the finer shades of selfhood so palpable to Buddhist eyes, long accustomed to the minutest psycho-spiritual analysis. Consequently her conception of self-will is in comparison gross (fine as it may be in its immediate Christian context), and her silence of the will not the ultimate silence of the will. If *Shūnyatā* is described as the absolute cessation of even the faintest vestige of self-consciousness or ego-sense, however, and if from the cessation of self-consciousness the cessation of self-will necessarily follows, then obviously it should be possible to regard the complete cessation of self-will as equivalent to the realization of *Shūnyatā*. Silence in its profoundest sense is thus *Shūnyatā* and *Shūnyatā* is the

Absolute Silence.

No less deep is the ultimate meaning of 'Voice'. In almost all religions and cultures the voice, speech, or utterance of man, as he expresses his thought in words, has been regarded as symbolizing the creation of the world by God, the involution of the spiritual into the material, the manifestation of the Absolute as the relative. *Shūnyatā*, the ultimate principle according to Buddhism, is not regarded as exercising creative functions: it is neither the First Cause nor the existential ground of things. But it would be a grave mistake to assume that it is therefore devoid of a dynamic aspect. This dynamic aspect is *karuṇā*, compassion. According to the Mahayana School, compassion is much more than an emotion. Three kinds of *karuṇā* are distinguished. In the words of Henri de Lubac, who prefers to render *karuṇā* by 'pity':

> The first sort of pity has as its object the beings who suffer; it is *sattvālambana karuṇā*—the ordinary, inferior kind of pity, tainted by the vulgar error of believing in the reality of living beings. The second sort, which is higher, has as its object painful sensations themselves; this is *dharmālambana karuṇā* [phenomena, including sensations, are technically known as *dharma* in Buddhist philosophy][7] and the person who experiences it knows that beings do not exist, but only their *dharma* [or constituent psycho-physical phenomena]. But this is still only an approximation to true knowledge, for the painful sensations do not exist in or by themselves; and so this second sort of pity still involves *āvidyā* (nescience). There must therefore be a third kind of pity—pure pity, the pity which has no object; *anālambana karuṇā*. A virtue is all the higher, the more it is in this sense pure. Perfect pity, ideal pity—'the great pity'—will therefore arise, not from the love of creatures nor to put an end to suffering, but quite

gratuitously, from the love of pity itself. And, at this highest level, just as it is no longer directed towards any living being or any reality, so it is not the possession of any particular person.[8]

It is of this third kind of *karuṇā* that *The Voice of the Silence* itself speaks in the well-known passage, 'Compassion is no attribute. It is the Law of LAWS—eternal Harmony. . .'[9] Strictly speaking, Compassion, in this sense, is no more an aspect of *Shūnyatā* than it is an attribute of the thinking, feeling self. To describe it as an aspect of *Shūnyatā* means in effect to assert that, unlike *Shūnyatā*, which possesses independent reality, Compassion possesses merely dependent or derivative reality, which in turn implies the assertion that it is not fully real. A number of Mahayana texts make it clear that *Shūnyatā* is as much an aspect of *Karuṇā* as *Karuṇā* is of *Shūnyatā*. In fact in the *Dharmakāya*, or whole Body of Reality in the ultimate sense, *Shūnyatā* and *Karuṇā*, the conditioned and the Unconditioned, *Samsara* and *Nirvana*—in fact all possible pairs of logically contradictory terms—are related in a manner inconceivable to the intellect, so that the relation cannot be described in terms of unity or of difference, nor yet in terms of neither unity nor difference. Only from the purely relative standpoint is it permissible to speak of *Shūnyatā* manifesting as *Karuṇā*, or of one being static, the other dynamic, as though they were two distinct or even distinguishable entities. Both transcend the reach of logic. The only way in which their relationship can be described is by some such paradoxical, that is to say logically contradictory, expression as 'The Voice of the Silence'. Speaking again from the relative standpoint, it may be said that the fact that these precious fragments from 'The Book of the Golden Precepts' bear such a profoundly paradoxical title may be taken as an indication that they emanate from, and are intended to help the disciple attain to, a state beyond the power of reason to describe.

The contents of *The Voice of the Silence* are, in parts, no less paradoxical than is its title. Only two examples will be given here, the reader, we believe, preferring to enjoy the excitement of discovering and studying others for himself.

In Fragment I the neophyte is warned, 'Thou canst not travel on the Path until thou hast become that Path itself'.[10] The path referred to is of course the spiritual path. In all religions, but perhaps most of all in Buddhism, where the figure of The Way reigns supreme, is the spiritual life depicted as a progression through a series of stages—the first lying beneath one's feet, the last glimmering hardly discernible through the mists of the far distance—and the spiritual aspirant as a pilgrim or traveller. While the analogy has many advantages, as its world-wide popularity attests, it is by no means exempt from the danger that dogs every metaphor employed to elucidate religious or philosophical themes—the danger of being understood too literally and too logically, so that it becomes not the stimulus of a spiritual response but merely the starting point of a chain of deductions. In the present case, the danger lies in pushing the metaphor of the path so far as to think that because, in actual fact, the path and the traveller on the path are two different entities the spiritual path and the spiritual aspirant are two different entities too. From this there follows a conclusion diametrically opposed to the fundamental principles of Buddhism—the conclusion that just as the traveller, from the beginning to the end of his journey, remains unchanged in relation to the portions of the road over which he travels, so the self or ego or principle of personal identity persists unchanged as it passes through the succession of spiritual experiences or stages intercalated between the mundane starting point and the transcendental goal. Against this perfectly logical but absolutely wrong deduction the paradoxical statement that, in reality, you cannot travel the Path until you have become that Path itself launches a vigorous protest.

As all schools of Buddhism maintain, the idea of an unchanging soul or self or *ātman* distinct from the various mental processes is a delusion, in fact the greatest of all delusions, so that only from the standpoint of relative or conventional truth is it possible even to speak of the attainment of Nirvana by this or that person. Spiritual progress consists not in the acquisition of spiritual attainments by the ego as though they were a species of personal property, but in the attenuation of the ego, or rather of the false idea of egohood, in such a way that from gross it becomes subtle, from subtle more subtle still, until in the end the aspirant becomes as it were an impersonal stream of spiritual energy which, becoming progressively wider and deeper, eventually discovers that it coincides with the fathomless ocean of Nirvana. By its paradoxical identification of Path and pilgrim *The Voice of the Silence* in effect reminds us that just as the 'individual' or 'person' is merely a name for certain psychosomatic states, so 'Path' is no more than a convenient designation for a succession of thoughts, words, and deeds oriented in the direction of 'Enlightenment'. Whether at a higher or a lower level, there is in reality no question of personal acquisition at all.

This links up with the vitally important teaching, found in Fragment II, concerning 'The Two Paths'. These are the path of the Shravaka and the Pratyekabuddha, on the one hand, and that of the Bodhisattva on the other. In *The Voice of the Silence* the first is called 'The Open Path' and 'The Path of Liberation', the second 'The Secret Path', 'The Path of Renunciation', and 'The Path of Woe'. According to the popular interpretation, the difference between the two paths is that while one aims at individual emancipation the other aims at universal emancipation. Whereas the Shravaka is content to become an Arahant, to gain Nirvana for himself alone, the Bodhisattva is not satisfied unless he achieves

Supreme Buddhahood, for in this case he will be able to lead a multitude of other beings to Nirvana. But as we have already pointed out, Nirvana is not something that can be owned, either individually or collectively. The Bodhisattva's renunciation of the Open Path, the path of personal liberation, is therefore not to be construed as meaning that this path represents an actually realizable possibility. What it means is that the Bodhisattva resists the temptation of thinking of Nirvana as a personal acquisition. In *Prajñāpāramitā* language, he realizes that Nirvana is to be attained by means of a non-attainment. With this lapse into paradox we remind ourselves that, after all, of all methods of giving expression to transcendental realities that of logical contradiction is perhaps the safest and least open to misunderstanding. A metaphor may be taken literally, a paradox never. Without some appreciation of the reason why *The Voice of the Silence* gives so profoundly paradoxical a twist to the time honoured figure of The Way we shall be able to understand neither the message of this marvellously meaningful little treatise nor the implications of the Bodhisattva Ideal.

Our second example of the use of paradox in *The Voice of the Silence* is taken from the end of Fragment III, where the Bodhisattva, now on the threshold of Enlightenment, is told:

> . . . If thou would'st be Tathagata, follow upon thy predecessor's steps, remain unselfish till the endless end.[11]

This is profound doctrine, but we are not now concerned with the passage as a whole but only with the paradoxical phrase with which it concludes. It is no mere coincidence that the expression 'the endless end' should have been used in association with unselfishness of the most exalted kind—the unselfishness of a Tathagata or Buddha.

Now there are some who understand Nirvana so crudely as to imagine that it does in the gross literal sense stand at the end of the spiritual path, as it were waiting to be reached, or realized, by the aspirant. Besides bringing Nirvana, which is eternal (*dhruvā*) in the sense that it transcends time, within the time-series, such literal-mindedness in effect commits the far graver mistake of treating Nirvana as though it could in reality be the object of personal attainment and possession. As we have already shown at sufficient length in the case of the first paradox, that of the Path, the Bodhisattva does not and cannot treat Nirvana as a personal possession, for it is of his very essence to have transcended those false notions of absolute selfhood, of real personal identity, upon which the idea of possession is necessarily grounded. Since he is incapable of thinking of Nirvana as a possession, or as being in the ultimate sense an attainment, the Bodhisattva cannot regard it as in reality constituting the end of his career. We do not wish to labour the point, for to those who followed the previous paragraph with attention it will already be sufficiently obvious: *The Voice of the Silence* speaks of 'the endless end' for what is basically the same reason that it speaks of the pilgrim becoming the Path. Adopting a slightly different point of view, however, it may be said by way of supplementary explanation that if, to speak in accordance with the relative truth, the attainment of Wisdom is the 'end' of the Bodhisattva's career, that end is 'endless' because Wisdom is ultimately non-different from Compassion which has for object the uninterrupted succession of birth, old age, disease, and death in the *Samsara* which, as a process, is without end.

From paradoxes we pass to poetry. The poetry of *The Voice of the Silence* is in places as beautiful as its paradoxes are startling. By poetry we do not mean verse, for in their English dress, at least, these inspired utterances fail to observe the rules of classical prosody. But what is poetry? For the purposes of our present discussion—enough ink has already been spilled in attempts to define the indefinable—we shall take it that the essence of poetry is imagery. The poetic image, or more simply the image, is defined as 'anything concrete or abstract introduced figuratively to represent something which it strikingly resembles, as sleep for death.' Imagery, of whatever kind, is thus based on comparison. Not on any kind of comparison, however. An image is made only when the objects compared are of different kinds but possessed of the same attributes. Thus in the case of the metaphor 'golden sunset' we compare a phenomenon of sun and clouds and sky with a metal because, though the objects are of quite different kinds, they share a common quality, in this case, a colour.

Despite the fact that in its decline poetry, or what by courtesy continues to be styled poetry, either uses the old figures of speech mechanically or manufactures new ones artificially, the comparisons between one object and another which constitute as it were the life-blood of the image are not arbitrary. In the section, 'Transition to the Tantra' of *A Survey of Buddhism*[12] we tried to show how the sacramental action of the Tantras was based on the *Avataṁsaka Sūtra*'s conception of the universe as a gigantic system of correspondences. The poetic image is similarly based. And just as the efficacy of the sacramental action of the Tantras is ultimately due to the essential truth of the Sutra's teaching, so does the power of the image to induce poetic experience ultimately derive from the fact that its comparisons are not merely fanciful but strike deep root into the very nature of things.

Images are perceptions of real correspondences. These correspondences the true poet—not the mere versifier or wearer of poetic reach-me-downs— perceives intuitively. The intuitive perception of a correspondence through an image constitutes poetic truth. It is because they possess the power of perceiving correspondences, or imagination in the Blakean sense, that the great poets of the world are not merely 'the idle singers of an empty day' but 'the hierophants of an unapprehended mystery'. Not unoften, indeed, are we delighted by the discovery that there is more Soul-wisdom in the pages of the poets than in those of the academic philosophers and the professionally devout. The poet, as the Romantics clearly saw, and as Carlyle so magnificently dinned into the ears of an unbelieving generation, is a prophet and a seer. Hence we need not be surprised to find that the prophets and seers are poets. The Vedic rishis, the authors of the poetical books of the Old Testament, and the Sufis of medieval Iran, were poets as true as any that ever breathed. Mohammed, Christ, and the Buddha—to go higher still in the scale of spiritual attainment—all made extensive use of metaphor and simile in their teachings. That this should be so is undoubtedly due to the fact that images based on a system of correspondence are more easily able to arouse the imagination, to stimulate the intuition, or (to revert to the term beloved of our present text) to awaken Soul-wisdom, than more rational methods.

Hence *The Voice of the Silence* abounds in imagery. One can hardly turn a page without encountering at least one strikingly beautiful figure of speech. What could be more vigorous than the image in which it is said that the Disciple's sins '. . . will raise their voices like as the jackal's laugh and sob after the sun goes down; . . .'[13] or more vivid than the picture of the Hosts of Souls hovering bird-like over 'the stormy sea of human life',[14] or more solemnly beautiful than the simile which says of the newly arisen Buddha that He stands

> . . . like a white pillar to the west, upon whose face the rising Sun of thought eternal poureth forth its first most glorious waves.[15] ?

Examples could be multiplied indefinitely. An assiduous student might well compile for *The Voice of the Silence*, as E. M. Hare has done for the *Sutta-Nipāta*,[16] an Index of Similes.

But imagery, though the essence of poetry, is not the whole of it. Other elements are also needed. For instance, rhythm. Though it is nowadays generally admitted that poetry can dispense with metre and rhyme, it would be difficult to imagine it existing without some kind of rhythm, either regular or irregular. This may well be because rhythm is essentially a periodicity, a reflection of sameness and difference within the order of time, and as such indirectly in correspondence with imagery, their reflection in words. Be that as it may (for it is no more than a speculation), there is no doubt that the poetry of *The Voice of the Silence* is strongly rhythmical and that its marvellous effects are owing, in some cases at least, as much to rhythm as to imagery. Consider, for instance, the following sublime passage, arranged in stanza form so that the reader may be the better able to appreciate how strongly, indeed regularly, rhythmical it is:

Let thy Soul lend its ear
To every cry of pain
Like as the lotus bares its heart
To drink the morning sun.

Let not the fierce Sun dry
One tear of pain before
Thyself has wiped it
From the sufferer's eye.

But let each burning human tear
Drop on thy heart and there remain;
Nor ever brush it off, until
The pain that caused it is removed.[17]

The prosodist will observe that the stanzas scan perfectly. In the first stanza two iambic trimeters are succeeded by two iambic tetrameters, the second is composed of trimeters and dimeters, while the glorious third stanza consists of four iambic tetrameters.

That merely rhyme should be needed to make this 'poem of pity' acceptable not only as poetry but as perfectly good traditional English verse is no accident. Shelley in an inspired moment spoke of 'the incantation of this verse'. All great poetry is incantation. It produces its effect more by sound than by meaning. The classic illustration of this profound truth is the famous first line of Keats' *Endymion*: 'A thing of beauty is a joy forever'. According to a story, probably apocryphal, Keats originally wrote, 'A thing of beauty is a constant joy' and showed the line to his friend Leigh Hunt, whom it failed to satisfy. Keats thereupon thought again and wrote the line previously quoted. The difference in meaning between the two lines is negligible; both are iambic pentameters; but one is poetry, the other prose. Why so tremendous a difference? The answer can lie only in the fact that whereas the meaning is the same the associated sounds, including the respective rhymes of the two lines, are different. A Poem is a kind of mantra. We might even say that while imagery is the content of poetry, the mantra is its form. Indeed, just as poetry can sometimes substitute a meaning for an image and still remain poetry by retaining its mantraic form, so it can substitute meaning for mantraic quality and remain poetry in that case too. In other words, though poetry in the fullest sense combines image, mantra, and meaning, a combination of image and mantra, or of meaning and mantra, alone, is also poetry. Meaning by itself is prose; the addition of metre merely condemns it to be verse. Such distinctions should not, however, be mistaken for divisions. A poem, as we have insisted in 'Advice to a Young Poet', is a whole, and its 'parts' though distinguishable are inseparable.[18]

In passages like the one quoted above, which is one of the loftiest peaks of that Himalayan range of spiritual truths that is *The Voice of the Silence,* all the constituents of poetry in the full sense of the term are present. It is as though whenever it has anything of special importance to impart, the text either explodes in paradox or erupts into the imagery and starts shaking with the mantra-like vibrations of poetry. The fact that *The Voice of the Silence* consists of, or at least contains, what are really mantras in English, incidentally may account for the circumstance that as a whole it does not correspond to any known Tibetan text, though individual verses seem to have been identified. For as an eminent Tibetologist has suggested to the writer, if the translator of these three fragments from 'The Book of the Golden Precepts' was as much concerned to reproduce the mantraic effect of the original as to translate its literal meaning she may well have found some sacrifice of the letter to the spirit of the text inevitable.

The Voice of the Silence is not, however, all paradox and poetry—a mercy for which the weakness of human nature is doubtless sufficiently thankful. Little valleys of rationality and prose do intervene, for even the Himalayas are not all peak and precipice. But as he rests in them between bouts of spiritual mountaineering even the most casual reader should remember that the message of *The Voice of the Silence* is not to be understood unless we realize that it appeals to the heart, that it strives to develop intuition, to awaken Soul-wisdom, and that in so doing its principal methods are paradox and poetry.

Notes

The Meaning of Buddhism and the Value of Art

1. *The Complete Works of Swami Vivekananda* (seventh edition, Advaita Ashrama, Mayavati, Almora, U. P.), pp. 2—3
2. *The Republic of Plato* Translated by J. L. Davies and D. J. Vaughan (Macmillan, London, 1923), pp. 235—37
3. *Udāna* VI, 4, F. L. Woodward, *Some Sayings of the Buddha* (Oxford University Press), pp. 286—88
4. *The Meaning of Art* (Penguin), p. 70
5. *Letters of Sri Aurobindo, (On Poetry and Literature)* third series (Sri Aurobindo Circle, Bombay, 1949), p. 4
6. *ibid*, p. 285
7. *ibid*, p. 287
8. *ibid*, p. 289
9. *ibid*, p. 292—93
10. For a discussion of the first three terms, see Rhys Davids, *Dialogues of the Buddha* I, p. 7
11. *Letters of Sri Aurobindo* (third series), p. 296
12. *Dialogues of the Buddha* II, p. 300—4
13. *The Book of the Kindred Sayings (Saṃyutta Nikāya)* Part I, Kindred Sayings with verses (Sagatha-vagga), translated by Mrs Rhys Davids, assisted by Suriyagoda Sumangala Thera (Pali Text Society, London) p. 247

14. *ibid*, pp. 245—46
15. *Dialogues of the Buddha* II, p. 103
16. *The Four Essential Doctrines of Buddhism* (Colombo, 1948), p. 155

The Religion of Art

1. Dent, *Stories, Essays and Poems* (Everyman's Library), p. 284
2. *ibid.*, p. 260
3. F. L. Woodward, *Some Sayings of the Buddha* (Oxford University Press), pp. 92—93
4. Luzac, *The Doctrine of Awakening* (London), p. 5
5. *Some Sayings of the Buddha*, p. 316
6. *ibid.*, p. 285
7. *Requiem and Other Poems* Translated from the German with an Introduction and Notes by J. B. Leishman, (Hogarth Press, London, 1949), p. 115
8. *The Meaning of Art* (Penguin, 1951), p. 64
9. *Requiem and Other Poems*, p. 149
10. *Prometheus Unbound* Act IV, 11. 477—78
11. *The Aryan Path* (Bombay, August 1953), p. 345
12. *ibid.*
13. *Requiem and Other Poems* Introduction, p. 47
14. Rainer Maria Rilke, *Later Poems* (Hogarth Press, 1938), p. 243
15. *Par l'operation d'un mystere vengeur*
Dans la brute assoupi un ange se reveille.
(Baudelaire, L'aube spirituelle.)
16. Bhagavan Dhas, *Science of the Emotions* (third edition, Theosophical Publishing House, Adyar, Madras, 1924), p. 218
17. *Buddhism as Personal Religion* (Colombo), pp. 8—9

18. Rainer Maria Rilke, *Briefe aus Muzot,* pp. 83—84 (Quoted in *Sonnets to Orpheus.* The German text, with an English Translation, Introduction and Notes by J. B. Leishman, (Hogarth Press, 1949) Introduction, p. 13
19. 'The Relativity of Perfection', *Stepping Stones* vol. 1, no. 6 (Kalimpong), pp. 135—36
20. *English Critical Essays, (Nineteeth Century)* selected and edited by Edmund D. Jones (Oxford University Press), p. 218
21. 'Art and Mortality', *Four Essays on Art and Painting* (Bureau of Current Affairs, London), p. 9
22. *Some Sayings of the Buddha,* pp. 193
23. *Music at Night* (Penguin, 1950), p. 87
24. *Critique of Judgement* sect. 29 (Quoted by Will Durant, *The Story of Philosophy,* 1952, p. 279)
25. *Selected Essays* (Penguin, 1950), pp. 118—19
26. *The Meaning of Art,* p. 70
27. Arts and the Man, *A Short Introduction to Aethetics* (New American Library, 1951), p. 218
28. *English Critical Essays,* p. 115
29. *Arts and the Man,* p. 49
30. Carlyle, 'The Hero as Poet', *English Critical Essays,* p. 220
31. *The Meaning of Art,* p. 30
32. 'Why Modern Poetry is Obscure', Second talk, *The Listener* (London, 12 March 1953)

Paradox and Poetry in The Voice of the Silence

1. Sangharakshita, *A Survey of Buddhism* (Indian edition), pp. 317—20
2. p. 27. All references are to the *verbatim* reprint published by Theosophy Co. (India) Private Ltd., 40 New Marine Lines, Bombay 1
3. *A Survey of Buddhism*, pp. 348—64
4. Edward Conze, *Selected Sayings from the Perfection of Wisdom*, p. 79
5. *Selected Sayings*, p. 105
6. *Some Sayings of the Buddha*, p. 94
7. Additions in brackets are by the present writer.
8. *Aspects of Buddhism* (1943), p. 40. Henri de Lubac does not reveal the source of this classification
9. *ibid*, pp. 75—76
10. *The Voice of the Silence*, p. 14
11. p. 78
12. pp. 406—12
13. *The Voice of the Silence*, p. 17
14. *ibid*, p. 9
15. *ibid*, p. 71
16. *Woven Cadences of Early Buddhists*, pp. 181—82
17. p. 14
18. *The Aryan Path* (August 1953), p. 345